The
MASTER
BOOK
of
CANDLE
BURNING

or

HOW TO BURN CANDLES
FOR EVERY PURPOSE

ORIGINAL PUBLICATIONS

BRONX, N.Y.

All rights to this book have been purchased from Marvel Book Co.

Published in **1984** by:

ORIGINAL PUBLICATIONS
Div. Jamil Products Corporation

2486 Webster Avenue
Bronx, New York 10458

©1984 ORIGINAL PUBLICATIONS

ISBN 0·942272·06·4

PREFACE

In order to understand the full siginficance of Candle Burning one must go back to the very beginnings of mankind, but to attempt a *complete* history of Fire Worship would require a lifetime of research and would fill many volumes.

Such a history would require an historical outline of seven great religions extant today (Hinduism, Buddhism, Zoroastrianism, Confucianism, Judaism, Christianity and Mohamedanism as well as many religious sects and cults of lesser importance in the world scene.

A book of this kind would have little *popular* value because those who are interested in the Philosophy of Fire and who wish to know more about the Art of Candle Burning and its application to their daily lives ask only one question: "How can *I* burn candles in a manner which will bring me the most satisfaction and consolation?"

In order to answer that question it is necessary to eliminate all technical, dry and often times torturous historical background. It is necessary to sift and sort every fact, scrutinize every detail, search for the kernel.

It is to be hoped that this volume answers that question in a manner which is satisfactory to the reader. It has been necessary, of course, to include some historical data and other anthropological data in order to better illustrate the symbolism involved in modern candle burning as practised by so many people today.

This data has been accumulated from many sources; it has been culled from literally hundreds of books and articles.   The modern rituals outlined here are based upon practices which have been described by mediums, spiritual advisors, evangelists, religious interpreters, neologists and others who should be in a position to know.

It has been the author's desire to interpret and explain the basic symbolism involved in a few typical exercises so that the reader may recognize this symbolism and proceed to develop his own symbolism in accordance with the great beauty and highest ethics of the Art.

New York, N. Y. 1942   *Henri Gamache*

CHAPTER I

The PHILOSOPHY OF FIRE

It makes little difference what your religion may be — candle burning brings consolation and solace. Candle Burning perhaps better illustrates the UNIVERSALITY of MAN than any other thing.

It has been said of religion that everything new in it is *old* and everything old in it is *new* and I say that this is true for there has been no NEW RELIGION SINCE THE BEGINNING OF THE WORLD!

Within all men and women there is an intuitive sense of God. In each of us is a sense of human weakness and dependence, a distinction between Good and Evil, the hope of a better life, the belief in an Omnipotent Guiding Will in the world and universe.

These basic elements and truths have been with us as far back as we can trace the history of mankind.

Even St. Augustine said that what we call the Christian religion only began to be *called* "Christian" after the coming of Jesus Christ — that the religion itself existed even among the ancients long before Christ.

When we understand that simple thought — we can understand WHY the Philosophy of Fire, or Fire Worship, has been a part of every great religion since man emerged from caves and came into God's light of day!

The foundation of Fire Worship is in God and no man can say it is a heathen practice who has given it any consideration. Its symbolism is Purity itself!

That we may better understand Fire Worship or the Philosophy of Fire let us go back to the beginning and ask "How did Fire Worship originate?" When we find this answer we find the key to the symbolism of modern Candle Burning.

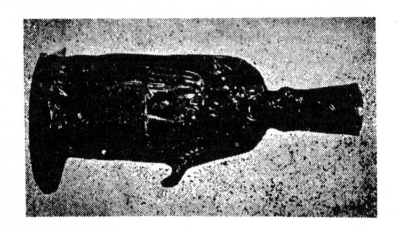

GUARDIAN-TYPE Candle Representing ancient priest in flowing robes. About "" High.

CHAPTER II

ORIGIN of FIRE WORSHIP

No one knows who invented fire .... or rather its first practical application to the needs of man. Perhaps the first fire was taken from a volcano; or from a raging forest fire which had been started by lightning. In any case, primitive man learned that fire kept him warm and dry and made his food more satisfying to his taste. Because life was hard. his appreciation for fire was far greater than is ours. He guarded it carefully, lest the winds, the rains and the elements put it out! It kept the wild beasts of the forests from his door. No wonder it was a mighty influence in his life. No wonder it was a portent of disaster when it went out! No wonder he saw in this fire a resemblance to the Sun which was so welcome to him since he then could face his natural enemies unafraid!

What was more natural, then, than that he should give praise to the sun, and he should worship it as *his* Savior? And was it not logical that in the same way he should consider the fire in his hearth no less divine?

Thus, from this humble beginning, man began his worship of Fire. The custom was not confined to any one particular group, nor did it spring up and thrive on any one continent. All races, in many climes, of all complexions adopted the custom and changed it only in small ways to meet their particular needs.

According to W. S. Blackman, "Fire is sometimes looked upon as a benign agent, sometimes as a purifying agent, sometimes as a destroying demon. It purifies and warms and heals. It protects the new born child and lights up the road for the departing spirit. It drives off evil influences, destroys disease, makes the sun shine, stops rain from falling. It plays a large and important part both in the religious and social life of all races of mankind from the cradle to the grave!"

We have read how primative man kept his fire lighted at the mouth of his cave to ward off wild beasts. It can be readily understood then, that as late as 4000 years later, fire was still looked upon as the *symbol of protection.*

W. Grant Stewart relates that Scotch Highlanders used fires to ward off witches so that their herds might not become infected and ill.

W. Mannhardt is the authority for many German folk tales and traditions wherein he describes the use of fire for similar purposes in Central Europe.

Gradually, this symbolism of "warding off evil" took on a rather different aspect. Fire became a purifying agent. Direct contact with it was thought to drive out any devils within the person and to cleanse or purify them.

For example, among the Parisees at one time, when a man died his widow was said to be contaminated with the same evils which had taken her husband's spirit away. Thus she was led to a low platform under which a fire was built. Here the unfortunate woman had to remain for an hour each day for thirty days at the end of which time it was thought that the evil spirits had left her body and she was again pure.

In a like manner among the Parisees, when a child was born a candle was kept burning somtimes for ten days, sometimes for forty full days or the confinement period.

In Britain, in Scandinavia and in Germany, several candles were lighted around a new born infant to keep it from falling into the power of evil spirits, according to Blackman.

Many of these customs are still followed today even though in some cases, centuries have passed since they were originated.

Perhaps the greatest exponents of Fire Worship have been the Parisees or Zoroastrians who worshipped not in temples but in the open air. They abominated images and idols and worshipped the Sun and Fire as *Representative of the Omnipresent Diety*! Their only church or temple was a round tower in which a sacred fire was kept burning at all times. Usually these fire temples were located on a hill top and the faithful worshipped in the open air.

The story is told of an unbeliever who approached a Parisee Fire Temple and beheld the sacred fire which was never allowed to die out. "What!" he exclaimed to the priest in charge, "do you worship the fire?" "Not the fire", the priest replied, "it is to us the emblem of the sun and his genial warmth"

This custom seems to have been general from earliest antiquity and such fires were maintained constantly because the God's presence was thought to lie therein.

———

CHAPTER III

A FEW BIBLICAL REFERENCES SUBSTANTIATING THE PHILOSOPHY OF FIRE

The idea of a Fire God was not a belief of the Zoroastrians alone for Moses told his people that their God was "a *consuming* fire "

Does not the Bible say that God appeared in the Cherubim over the gates of Eden as a Flaming Sword — and to Abraham as Flame of Fire and to Moses as a Fire in the bush at Horeb?

If we refer to 1 Kings, Chapt. 18, we read:

36 And it came to pass at the time of the offering of the evening sacrifice, that Elijah the Prophet came near, and said, LORD, God of Abraham, Isaac and of Israel, let it be known this day that thou *art* God of Israel, and that I am thy servant, and that I have done all these things at Thy Word.

37 Hear me, OH LORD, hear me; that this people may know that Thou art the Lord God, and that thou hast turned their heart back again.

38 Then the fire of the LORD fell, and consumed the burnt sacrifice and the wood, and the stones and the dust and licked up the water that was in the trench.

39 And when all the people saw it they fell on their faces: and they said, the LORD, he is the God; the LORD, he is the God.

Again in the Second Book of Chronicals, Chapt. 7, we read:

1. Now when Solomon had made an end of praying, the fire came down from heaven, and consumed the burnt offering and the sacrifices; and the glory of the LORD filled the house

2. And the priests could not enter the house of the LORD because the Glory of the LORD had filled the LORD'S house.

In the Biblical passage last quoted we find a modern counterpart for there are many people who keep a vigil light burning constantly in their homes that it may be filled with a beneficence which will keep out all negative or evil influences.

With such authority as the Bible behind it, it is not to be wondered at that Candle Burning has become such an important part in the lives of many people today.

Again the reader is referred to the Bible. This time to HABAKKUK, Chapt. 3:3-5 verse. Here is a prayer which will elevate anyone who reads it:

3 God came from Teman, and the Holy One From Mount Paran. Selah. His glory covered the heavens, and the earth was full of his praise.

4. And his brightness was as the light; and he had horns coming out of his hand and there was the hiding of his power.

5. Before him went the pestilence and burning coals went forth at his feet.

There are many who interpret this prayer as one to overcome ill health and who read the prayer over and over each day, the meanwhile burning candles of a color to harmonize with the condition to be overcome. (This subject is discussed in Chapter 5 of this book).

For those who wish to follow the Philosophy of Fire, the author refers the reader to LEVITICUS 23, 1-13 and LEVITICUS 24, 1-7.

In these passages it is related that the Lord spoke unto Moses and admonished him to make an offering of fire FOR SEVEN DAYS. There are many who follow this custom by burning a SEVEN DAY CANDLE and reading the two above mentioned chapters each day for seven days.

Study the Gospel according to ST. JOHN, Chapt. 1, 1-10 verse:

1. In the beginning was the word, and the word was with God, and the word was God.

2. The same was in the beginning with God.

3. All things were made by him: and without him was not anything made that was made.

4. In him was life; and the life was the LIGHT OF MEN.

5. And the Light shineth in darkness and the darkness comprehended it not.

6. There was a man sent from God, whose name was John.

7. The same came for a witness, to bear witness of the Light; that all men through him might believe. — etc.

This passage has been interpreted by many as saying that there are good things all about us; there is a plentitude of gifts, of food, of health and happiness, of goodness and peace of mind. All these things are under our very noses but we perceive them not — or seeing them, understand them not.

Those who interpret the passage in this manner, burn candles that the "light of understanding" may enter into their hearts and minds, that they may better perceive the WAY of LIGHT and GAIN THE BLESSINGS WHICH THE LORD MEANT FOR EACH OF US TO HAVE AND ENJOY.

One who has followed the Philosophy of Fire recommends burning candles in the shape of a cross. The colors are based upon PLANETARY tables, each color being assigned to the days of the week as follows:

Sunday— burn a yellow candle in the shape of a cross
Monday— burn a white candle in the shape of a cross
Tuesday— burn a red candle in the shape of a cross
Wednesday— burn a purple candle in the shape of a cross
Thursday— burn a blue candle in the shape of a cross
Friday— burn a green candle in the shape of a cross
Saturday— burn a black candle in the shape of a cross

Read: Gospel According to JOHN: Chapters 1 and 5 each day.

CHAPTER IV

STRANGE CUSTOMS OF FIRE WORSHIP WITH MODERN COUNTERPARTS

A. Talbot in his famous writing "In the Shadow of the Bush", relates strange customs which have prevailed in many parts of Africa from time immemorial. One of these is of particular interest to those who follow the Philosophy of Fire because it has its counterpart right in our midst.

He observed that among the Ekoi tribes of West Africa, a peculiar form of "divorce" is practiced. If a woman desires to free herself of her husband she does not discuss the matter with him for fear of reprisal on his part. While her husband is away working, she rakes out the fire and drenches it with water.

She then cuts off her hair after which she paints herself all over with white paint. Upon completion of this ritual she becomes a free woman. It is said that a peculiar and inexplicable psycological reaction occurs in that even if she changes her mind she can never return to her husband regardless of her husband's threats and protestations.

This custom has a parallel in America — a custom which prevails in many cities and towns. The belief is often expressed by some people that they are in a "crossed condition", that is that they are held back by some seemingly impossible obstacle which may be real or fancied. Sometimes the condition may be attributed to another individual who is thought to have designs against one.

In any case a symbolism not unlike that of the Ekoi maid is followed to overcome the condition. Four candles are used; one black candle and three white candles. All are lighted but care is exercised to light the black one last. See Fig. 1

Fig.1

position 1-1 — *White Crucifix Altar Candles dressed with Hi-Altar Brand Oil*

position 2 — *Black Candle or Weed of Misfortune Brand' Candle dressed with Confusion Brand Oil*

position 3 — *White Power Brand Candle dressed with Domination Brand Oil*

Then the affected one prepares a bath into which a Bathing oil is placed. The candles are allowed to burn only during the time of bathing and then are extinguished. The following is read each day:

JOB, Chapter 21:17-18 verse:

17. How oft is the candle of the wicked put out? And how oft cometh their destruction upon them. God distributeth sorrows in his anger.
18. They are as stubble before the wind and as chaff that the storm carrieth away.

This process is repeated for seven days, a different oil being used in the bath each day. At the end of this period it is said that the "crossed condition" has been removed.

It is not the intention of the author to commend or criticize such rites but merely to point out the similarity of this to the practice of the Ekoi Tribes, and to attempt to explain the symbolism involved.

In the case of the Ekoi wife, the fire was raked out and drenched with water. This symbolised the breaking of the marriage vows since the fire was symbolic of the home and since the woman's place is in the home, she naturally is the guardian of the fire. When she put out the fire she expressed symbolically, her revolt.

The painting of her body in white is a "purification" rite; white, being the symbolic color for purity. Thus upon completion of the ritual she was symbolically free.

The symbolism of the other case is explained as follows: — Black is the symbolic color of evil. Therefore the black candle is lighted. White is symbolic of purity so three white candles are lighted that their combined light might overpower the light of the single black candle.

The bathing process, like the painting ritual of the Ekoi girl, is a purification ritual and symbolizes the cleansing of all evil thoughts and impurities from the individual. The entire ritual is highly symbolic of the conquest of Good over Evil.

There are many other customs and practices involved in candle burning which are so wide-spread and so universally accepted by different races and nationalities as to preclude the possibility of coincidence.

For example Blackman's researches show that in many widely separated countries the spluttering candle has been a prediction of misfortune — a theory which is held in popular favor by many people today.

Curiously enough, just recently a correspondent told of a custom to obtain marriage omens, which is practised in Italy and even by emigres to America: If two leaves of Basil are placed upon a candle and burn away quietly, the marriage will be happy. If they crackle their lives will be filled with quarrels.

Standard Size Crucifix Altar Candles (4½" high) are available in white and black, also in colors representing each day of the week.

CHAPTER V

THE SYMBOLISM OF COLOR IN CANDLES

The ancient philosophers believed that colors gave off vibrations, which affected one favorably or adversely. To those who may find this difficult to understand or to those who may feel some doubt, we can give a simple parallel to illustrate the point.

If we play a chord upon a piano, the strings of the piano vibrate and thus give off a sound which may be either pleasing or displeasing to the ear. Sometimes it fairly sings . . . . sometimes it creates a harsh discord which unsettles the nerves.

In the same way colors set up vibrations and either cause a pleasing or displeasing effect. Interior decorators, artists and others who work with colors, know this to be true. Manufacturers of automobiles, cosmetics, dresses, etc. use colors which *please* and *soothe* the eye and thus help sell their products.

How often does a man say, "This red tie is my favorite". How many times have you known a woman to be "partial to blue" or some other color?

This *leaning toward* a color is due to harmonious vibrations which are given off by certain colors causing an unconscious psycological reaction on our part.

Remember we have said "harmonious vibrations". In other words the vibrations given off by the color must be attuned to our own *personal vibrations* . . . so that they blend and make a pleasing result.

There are many schools of thought concerning the symbolism of color and its influence upon the individual. However, perhaps the most popular opinion is that in regard to the usage of Astral colors.

Among the Astrologers, it is a well recognized principle that the actions of each person are governed by the Sign under which they were born. Each sign, in turn, is governed by certain planets and to each Sign have been assigned certain gems and colors which are said to be attuned to those born under each sign. These colors are known as ASTRAL COLORS. Below we give the generally accepted list of these colors. Where one color is stronger in its influence it is indicated with CAPITAL letters. The other colors are of secondary or lesser influence but still far more harmonious than any colors not mentioned under each sign.

TABLE 1

POPULARLY ACCEPTED ASTRAL COLORS
ACCORDING TO EACH SIGN

Sign	For those Born between	Astral Colors
Aries	Mar. 21 — Apr. 19	WHITE and rose pink.
Taurus	Apr. 20 — May 19	RED and lemon yellow.
Gemini	May 20 — June 18	red and LIGHT BLUE.
Cancer	June 19 — July 23	GREEN and russet brown.
Leo	July 24 — Aug. 22	red and GREEN.
Virgo	Aug. 23 — Sept. 21	GOLD and Black — speckled with blue dots.
Libra	Sept. 22 — Oct. 21	black, CRIMSON, light blue.
Scorpio	Oct. 22 — Nov. 20	GOLDEN BROWN and black.
Sagittarius	Nov. 21 — Dec. 20	gold. red, GREEN.
Capricorn	Dec. 21 — Jan. 19	GARNET, Brown, silver-gray, and black.
Aquarius	Jan. 20 — Feb. 18	BLUE, pink, Nile green.
Pices	Feb. 19 — Mar. 20	White, PINK, emerald green, black.

Study this list carefully and remember *your* most harmonious vibratory color. You perhaps will recognize that *your* color *has proven harmonious to you in the past without you realizing it!*

Those who follow the Philosophy of Fire recommend the burning of colored candles which are in harmony with the subject. Thus, if you were born between March 21st and April 19th WHITE is your most important vibratory color and you should place emphasis on the burning of WHITE CANDLES. Since rose pink is your *secondary* Astral Color, candles of this color should be burned also. These would be your PRIMARY CANDLES. Astral type Candles are available in authentic Astral colors and wherever possible those incorporating at least two astral colors should be used.

Any other candles burned by an Aries person should be used for the specific vibratory influence symbolised by its color. These specific influences will be found in TABLE II.

Just as there is "the language of flowers", so, too, have philosophers from time immemorial indicated "the language of colors". Today we refer to this symbolism as Vibratory Influences.

TABLE II

POPULARLY ACCEPTED SYMBOLISM OR VIBRATORY INFLUENCES OF COLORS

White .... Symbolizes Purity, Truth, Spiritual Strength, Power and Realization.

Red .... Symbolizes Love, Health and Vigor

Light Blue ...... Spiritual Understanding, Soothing, Happiness; Cool, Calm Collected Thoughts. The Power to Perceive, Protection

Dark Blue .... ACID, Depressing, Moody, Unfortunate, Subduing.

Green .... Money, Wealth, Financial Success, Good Crops or Harvest.

Gold (Yellow) .... The Color of Attraction, Magnetic Hypnotic, Captivating, Drawing, Fascinating, Persuasive, Charming, Alluring, Cheerfulness.

Greenish Yellow . . . Arouses such sensations as Jealousy, Sickness or Cowardice, Anger and Discord.

Crimson . . . . Same as red but slightly modified by the Gold vibrations.

Brown . . . . Neutral, Non-Specific, Wavering, Hesitating, Faltering, Uncertainty.

Golden Brown . . . . Counteracts all of the Brown vibrations:— thus ASSERTIVE, Definite, Sure, Unhesitating, Aggressive.

Garnet . . . . Same as Red — but some of the vibrations of Blue. Thus: Understanding Love, Strong healthy mind and thoughts, vigorous will to do things. Exciting.

Pink . . . . Success, Conqueror of Evil, Winner in Love, Clean Living, Honorable.

Black . . . . Sadness, Mourning, Evil, Objectionable.

Russet Brown Same as Golden Brown but with a touch of Red vibrations. Thus: Uncertainty in Love Affairs.

Silver or Gray . . . . The Black vibrations almost nullified. Symbolic of the Victory of Good over Evil.

Orange . . . . Since this is a combination of Yellow and Red you can expect a happy mixture of Vibrations from both primary colors. Thus: Nerve stimulant, brain clearing, mind builder, Encouraging, Adaptability to various moods. Personality: Courageous. Strong love or Active in financial matters.

Purple .... This is a combination of the primary colors Red and Blue. Therefore look for vibrations of the primary colors: Powerful for furthering Worldly Ambitions; Overcoming business obstacles, High Tension, High Power. A color which should be "taken in small doses"

CHAPTER VI

SUGGESTIONS FOR SELECTING THE RIGHT COLORED CANDLES TO CREATE SPECIFIC VIBRATORY INFLUENCES

In the preceding chapter we have seen how each person is affected by the vibratory influences of their Astral Colors. We also have Cataloged the various colors and indicated the popularly accepted symbolism associated with each color.

From these two basic Tables those who follow the Philosophy of Fire derive their formulae for the proper selection of Candles to create the correct vibratory influences to overcome every condition or to induce conditions to their liking.

In Chapter II we have pointed out a number of applications for Fire Worship based upon research by no less an authority than W. S. Blackman. In this era of modern homes and skyscraper apartments, it is of course not practical to utilize open altar fires as did the ancients so that the ritual of candle burning is used instead with no lessening of the effect, say devotees of this Philosophy.

These adherents to an ancient custom claim that candles may be burned for any of the following conditions:

- To Obtain Money
- To Win the Love of Man or Woman
- To Settle a Disturbed Condition in the Home
- To Obtain Work
- To Conquer Fear
- To Develop Understanding
- To Break up a Love Affair
- To Bring Confusion to Another Who is Thought to Have Caused Unfavorable Vibrations
- To Gain Prosperity
- To Change One's Luck
- To Develop Spiritual Understanding
- To Learn the Truth
- To Soothe and Quiet the Nerves
- To Regain or Retain Health
- To Gain Power Over Others
- To Arouse Discord or Anger or Jealousy in Another
- To Awaken Spiritual Understanding in Another
- To Protect Against Evil Influences
- To Stop Slander
- To Gain What One Desires
- To Win or Hold Happiness
- To Attain Success
- To Heal an Unhappy Marriage
- To Overcome a Bad Habit
- To Relieve Pressure by an Enemy

There are many other conditions which it is said may be neutralized or harmonized by the burning of the proper candles but the foregoing list is sufficient to indicate the diversity of purposes for which followers of the Philosophy of Fire utilize Candle Burning.

The uninitiated may well wonder what candles to burn in order to induce any specific vibration for any particular objective.

In a sense, the selection is largely a matter of individual interpretation on the part of the person involved *after* the selection of candles in the Astral Colors as indicated in TABLE I and the basic Symbolism of the colors as indicated in TABLE II.

A medium of experience knows almost instinctively which combination of colors to utilize without reference to Color Tables or Charts.

For example a medium might recommend the burning of GREEN CANDLES for all MONEY MATTERS. The explanation is as follows:—

If we refer to TABLE II we find that green is symbolic of Money, Wealth, Financial Success and Good Crops. Therefore Green Candles would be essential to creating the proper vibrations.

However. TABLE I is used to select the correct ASTRAL COLOR of Candles. If one is born between Oct. 22nd and Nov. 20th, Brown and Black candles would also be used. The medium in this case might possibly suggest the burning of *green* Candles together with Brown and Black Astral Candles for at least 1 hour eacl day for seven days.

However if it is desired to burn Candles *FOR AN-OTHER*, a slight variation must be observed. The ASTRAL CANDLES must *not* be in the color of the person who is burning them but should be *in the Astral Color of the person for whom the candles are burned.* This would mean that the birth date of that person must be known and then the right ASTRAL colored candle used to create the correct vibrations harmonious to that person.

Based upon my research on the subject, I recommend that the candles be lighted early in the morning so that their light will be given strength as the sun increases in its brightness.

Some time ago I heard of the account of a young woman who felt pangs of Fear She had so many doubts about her ability to keep a job, to keep her husband's love. She felt that she was being harassed by unseen, hidden forces.

Questioning revealed that she was born on February 7th. This meant that *BLUE*, *Pink* and *Nile Green* were her ASTRAL COLORS. If we refer to TABLE II for the Symbolism of those colors we note that just the right vibrations are indicated to overcome this young woman's condition.

She was advised to obtain an Astral Candle in her colors and to burn it each evening after sundown.

The further recommendation was made that the Third Psalm of David be read thirty-three times at each burning. The Psalm follows:

> Lord, how they are increased that trouble me
> Many are they that rise up against me
>
> 2. Many there be which say of mv soul: There is no help for him in God. Selah.
>
> 3. But thou, O LORD, art a shield for me; my glory and the lifter up of mine head.
>
> 4. I cried unto the Lord with my voice, and he heard me out of his holy hill. Selah.
>
> 5. I laid me down and slept; I awaked; for the LORD sustained me.
>
> 6. I will not be afraid of ten thousands of people, that have set themselves against me round about.
>
> 7. Arise; O LORD: save me, O my GOD, for thou hast smitten all mine enemies upon the cheek bone; thou hast broken the teeth of the ungodly.
>
> 8. Salvation belongeth unto the LORD: thy blessing is upon thy people. Selah.

Perhaps ninety percent of the people who seek help have amatory difficulties. They desire the love of someone; they desire to regain a lost love; they bear a secret love for some one who is unaware of it; they feel they are losing the love of the husband or wife; their love is not returned by the object of their affections — and many similar adverse conditions of the heart.

In all such conditions I recommend meditation and prayer and suggest trying the Philosophy of Fire for its soothing influence. Try this:

— A PINK Candle is burned for two hours each day.
— An ASTRAL Candle in the *petitioner's* correct colors is burned with the PINK Candle.
  Two ASTRAL Candles in the *Loved One's* Astral Colors are burned with the other two candles.
  (See Exercise 4, Chapter 14, entitled, "To WIN THE LOVE OF MAN OR WOMAN")

In addition to the burning of the Candles as described, a small supply of Frankincense and Myrrh may be obtained and a little of this burned each day *after* burning the candles. While the Frankincense and Myrrh is burning, Chapter 6 of the Song of Solomon should be read if the petitioner is a *man* or Chapter 8 if the petitioner is a *woman.*

Those who are well versed in the Art of Candle Burning find that many people come to them asking why it is the Lord does not bring them more Success. They cannot get a job or else they cannot hold a job even when they do their work well. It seems that an evil spirit hovers over them keeping them from all the things that they feel they deserve.

They want SUCCESS — in all their undertakings. The want to expand and to accomplish all that they feel they are able and qualified to accomplish. Most petitioners in this class are bitter at the fact that Fate seems to hold them back.

In such conditions, I usually suggest the Success Formula of Candle Burning with ORANGE Candles and Candles in the ASTRAL Colors of the petitioner.

Reference to TABLE II will indicate why Orange Candles are suggested while TABLE I will give the proper color of candle to burn according to each Sign of the Zodiac. One candle of each color should be lighted each morning before going to look for a job. The 95th Psalm of David should be read and then the lights are smothered. Upon returning home in the evening the remainder of the two candles can be burned until entirely consumed. The process can be repeated as long as desired.

We could go on giving innumerable incidents and occasions like the above for burning candles but these few suffice to indicate how those who follow the Philosophy of Fire practice the Art of Candle Burning in this day and age.

CHAPTER VII

ALTAR and CANDLE STICKS

THEIR PLACE IN THE PHILOSOPHY OF FIRE

In the beginning, the Altar was the one place where primitive man could meet with God. He felt that he could not just offer up a sacrifice at any place that he might happen to be. He had to have a special place where the Almighty could come to receive the offering in the proper atmosphere

It had to be a place which was sanctified, purified, unpolluted and worthy of a visitation from the Omnipotent. Thus, even the earliest altar, as crude as they appear to be to us, were works of art in their time and made with loving care by these primitive peoples.

Early altars were made of earth or clay; sometimes stone was added; others were made entirely of stone. The law of Moses permitted altars of either clay and earth or of stone.

In every era these altars were adorned by fire or lights. Usually these lights took the form of clay or metal vessels in which a *vegetable* oil was placed with a wick. Animal oils such as tallow were never permitted. In fact it was considered a profane act to use animal oils of any kind. That is why, today, those who profess the Philosophy of Fire ALWAYS USE VEGETABLE OIL CANDLES or PARAFIN CANDLES.

In the Middle Ages the only occasion which called for the use of animal oil candles was the Black Mass which was secretely practised by certain Cultists in praise of Satan, the King of Darkness.

Why was earth or stone used for altars instead of some other material? Why was fire used to adorn these altars? What was the Symbolism involved?

If we refer to 1 Corinthians 5: 47-49 we find:
47. The first man is of the earth, earthy: the second man is the Lord from heaven.
48. As is the earthy, such are they also that are earthy: and as is the heavenly, such are they also that are heavenly.
49 And as we have borne the image of the earthy, we shall also bear the image of the heavenly.

Now, further to bear out the 47th verse quoted above we know that Adam was the first man and that the word

Adam means "red man", and that after the Fall of Eden he was called Adamah or *red earth*.

We have seen in previous chapters how primitive man saw in the Sun the symbolic representation of the Omnipotent . . . . and in Fire the symbolic representation of the Sun. Therefore fire on the altar symbolized the presence of God while the altar was symbolic of man himself.

As we know, there is but *one* true Altar, and that is our HEART upon which the light of Spiritual Understanding ever shines. Sometimes the light becomes dim, sometimes it fails — but if we wish to continue our spiritual growth we must keep the Light of Understanding and Love forever burning in our hearts.

There are scores of Biblical references to the altar, its manner of dressing, its location, its dedication, etc., and readers who are familiar with the Bible will readily recall them. The following are but a few of these references which we urge the reader to peruse:

```
GENESIS  8:20-21
ISAIAH 9: 2
ISAIAH 60: 1-5
ST. JOHN 8: 12
ST. LUKE 11: 33
LEVITICUS 8: 10-16
    "       8: 28
    "       9: 7-9
    "      10: 1-3
REVELATION 2: 1
```

In other passages of both the Old Testament and the New Testament we find that Altars were made of substances other than earth or stone. They were made of wood — for example of sandalwood or holywood. Some were made of other more commonly obtained woods and overlaid with gold. Some were studded with precious gems — but in every case there were Altar Lights or Candles constantly burning as a symbol of the Divine presence.

Today followers of the Philosophy of Fire do not concern themselves so much with the *material* from which the altar is made as they do in the ARRANGE-MENT and the Ritual of Observance at the Altar. This is called DRESSING THE ALTAR.

The Sanctification or Purification of the Altar is considered of prime importance and certain formulae are used by adherents, based upon instructions found in passages in the Bible.

For example some adherents believe that INCENSE is of importance in Altar Ritual and base their authority on the passage LEVITICUS 16:12-13.

12. And he shall take a censer full of burning coals of fire from off the altar before the LORD, and his hands full of sweet incense beaten small, and bring it within the vail.

13. And he shall put the incense upon the fire before the LORD, that the cloud of the incense may cover the mercy seat that is upon the testimony, that he die not.

Moderns do not follow this ritual exactly as stated in the passage quoted above. They find it impractical to use live coals upon the altar. Instead, Candles of a high quality are used.

A high quality of "ALTAR BRAND" incense may be used but it should be lighted *from the light of the candle which has been burning on the altar.*

Now let us discuss the matter of candle sticks. If we again refer to the Bible we find that the Lord gave very definite and specific instructions for making of candle sticks to be used in religious rites. (See EXODUS 25, 31-40)

These candle-sticks were to have been made of pure beaten gold with a central shaft. three branches out of one side and three branches out of the other side. Specific instructions were also given as to the design of the holders.

Now it is impossible to obtain a candle stick of this description today — for it would cost a king's ransom. Does this mean that followers of the Philosophy of Fire must be denied the right to worship as the Bible tells them?

The answer of course is an emphatic "no". Were they to deny themselves this sacred privilege they would be putting out the lights on the altars of their Hearts and we know that these must ALWAYS be kept burning at all costs in order to obtain salvation and the attainment of our desires.

We will illustrate herewith types of candlesticks which are commonly used by followers of the Philosophy of Fire. After all, the material from which the candle stick is made is of secondary importance, the important thing is the symbolism involved; the sincerity of purpose, the spark of divine inspiration which gives forth as the candles burn upon the altar.

Ordinarily, exponents of this form of worship state, the altar may be any place in the home which is secluded; a place where, when one is meditating or at prayer there is less likelihood of constant interruption. I suggest a simple solution to this problem as follows:

Set aside a place in the home that is quiet, where there will be no interruptions when in meditation and prayer. The attic, the basement, play room, the bedroom a spare room all are suitable for the purpose. It is not necessary to have a specially built altar as any space dedicated to this purpose *serves as the altar when the candles* are properly arranged.

Such an arrangement consists of a rectangular area such as a bureau top or a space of equal size. Two candle sticks are placed at the two back corners of this space and in them are inserted two white candles. Personally, I prefer using white Candles molded in the shape of a crucifix. They have their own base and require no candlestick holders . . . . and they are beautiful!

An Altar Cloth may be spread over the area thus described, if desired. This then comprises the altar.

Generally speaking, when burning Offeratory Candles of any specified color, they should be placed midway between the front and back of the altar. That is, along an imaginary center line. (See Fig. 2)

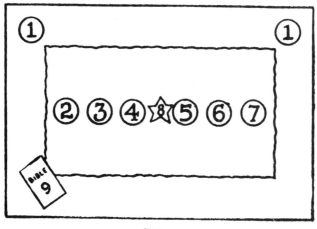

Fig. 2

No. 1-1 — Position of White Altar Candles (preferably in the symbolic shape of a crucifix).

No. 2, 3 & 4 — Positions of OFFERATORY CANDLES only. Burned for a specific purpose.

No. 5, 6 & 7 — Positions of ASTRAL CANDLES only — No Offeratory Candles are placed here.

No. 8 — Position of Incense Burner when used.

No. 9 — Position of Holy Bible.

With an arrangement such as we have described a beautiful altar of which you can be proud, will be the result.

Reference to Fig. 2 will show the position usually alloted to the Bible and to the Incense Burner.

When only one colored Offeratory candle is burned, it should occupy the Number 2 position while the incense burner occupies the Number 8 position.

When two colored Offeratory candles are burned they occupy No. 2 and No. 3 positions while the incense burner remains in No. 8 position. The Astral Candle occupies the No. 7 position unless there are two Astral Candles in which case use positions No. 7 and 6.

Some practitioners vary the ritual to some extent or expand it but the diagram given is the BASIC arrangement, generally speaking, and should be adhered to.

It should further be borne in mind that the Offeratory Candle (the candle which you have dedicated for some specific purpose) should always be on the LEFT — No. 2, 3 or 4 positions. Your ASTRAL Candle (based upon your own Astral colors) should be on the RIGHT or in No. 7, 6 or 5 positions unless other candles are used, in which case the Astral candle is grouped together with the Offeratory candles on the left. This will be illustrated further on in the text and particularly in Chapters XIV and XV where actual exercises are given with complete diagrams.

CHAPTER VIII

HOW TO DRESS A CANDLE
with SOME SUGGESTED DEVOTIONS

One of the most important factors in candle burning, according to many who follow the Philosophy of Fire, is DRESSING. As one adherent stated, many people believe that all that is necessary is to procure a candle of the right color and light it—and then every dream and wish will come true.

It is not as easy as all that, however. Anything worth having in life is worth striving for. Certain Rules must be followed. So it is with Candle Burning. Certain prescribed rules should be followed in trying to attain results.

Students of this line of thought believe that it is absolutely essential to anoint a candle with OIL and to impress upon it your most fervent wishes, so that it absorbs some of your vibrations — becomes almost a part of you . . . magnetized with your personality.

According to this school of thought, a candle has "polarity" the same as a magnet. It has a North Pole and a South Pole (See Fig. 3).

In annointing the candle with oil it is rubbed from the center *toward* the top or "North Pole" and from the center toward the bottom or "South Pole". The candle is never rubbed in both directions toward both poles.

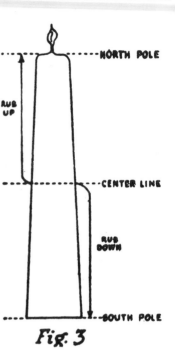

Fig. 3

As regards the selection of the oil to be used, this is a matter for the individual to decide for himself. There are many different types of oils but good judgement dictates that an oil should be selected whose vibrations are in harmony with the *color of the candle and the purpose for which the candle is to be burned.*

Among the many popular oils available for the above purposes are the following:

LODESTONE brand OIL

Fiery COMMAND brand OIL

DOMINATION brand OIL

Beneficial DREAM brand OIL

HI-ALTAR brand OIL

FIRE of LOVE brand OIL

GLOW of ATTRACTION brand OIL

ROSE of CRUCIFIXION brand OIL

CONQUERING GLORY brand OIL

INCENSE brand OIL

KINDLY SPIRIT brand OIL

ZODIAC brand OIL

BLACK ART brand OIL

HOLY BATH brand OIL

CONCENTRATION brand OIL

CLEOPATRA brand OIL

HINDU brand OIL
FIERY WALL of PROTECTION brand OIL
CRUCIBLE of COURAGE brand OIL
Flaming POWER brand OIL
DOVE'S BLOOD brand OIL
BIBLE brand OIL
COMPELLING brand OIL
CROWN of SUCCESS brand OIL
KING SOLOMON brand OIL
XX DOUBLE CROSS brand OIL
UNCROSSING brand OIL
Lady LUCK brand OIL
INFLAMMATORY CONFUSION brand OIL

It should be impressed upon the reader that the names used in connection with these oils are not to be construed as indicative of any use or guarantee in connection with them. The names simply indicate the impression that their particular aroma evoked in their maker's mind.

For example, Fire of Love Brand Oil has a peculiar fascinating fragrance which seems to conjure up memories of a passionate, fiery love. Domination Brand Oil seems to incite the senses so that the whole world seems at one's feet. Dream Brand Oil has a languorous odor that seems to be synonomous with dreams. Concentration Brand Oil has a pungent odor in which all the essences of the woods seem concentrated. So go these impressions. The symbolism in each case is a matter of individual discriminaton.

In the same manner, the use of any oil is a matter of individual selection. Usually it will be found that the 'right' oil is the same color as the 'right' color of candle or candles to be burned. There is a "follow through" of color harmony as regards both candle and oil. In the same manner the oil is selected which by its brand name is closest in harmony with the *purpose* for which the candles are burned.

For example, a follower of the Philosophy of Fire who was desireous of burning candles for the Success of a certain undertaking would place two white Altar Brand Crucifix Candles in the Number 1 positions. These would be dressed with Hi-Altar brand Oil. An ORANGE or Crown of Success brand candle would be selected and placed in the Number 2 position. This candle would be dressed with CROWN of SUCCESS brand OIL. Then the ASTRAL Candle of the worshipper would be placed in the Number 7 position and this would be dressed with ZODIAC brand OIL. (Astral Candles, regardless of the month or Sign are always dressed with Zodiac Brand Oil according to these students) The incense may be used or may be omitted as desired by the worshipper but if used I recommend that a high quality of Altar type incense be used rather than a cone or similar type commercial incense.

I suggest an hour's worship each evening accompanied by a reading and rereading of the 23rd Psalm of David during the period of devotion.

Sometime ago, I heard of a formula for those in a so-called "crossed condition". (See Fig. 4)

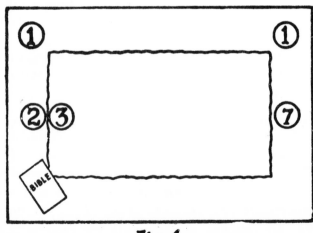

Fig. 4

Two WHITE candles (preferably of the shape of a crucifix) No. 1-1 positions dressed with Hi-Altar brand Oil.

One gray candle No. 2 position dressed with Uncrossing brand Oil.

One orange candle No 3 position dressed with Uncrossing brand Oil.

One Astral Candle No. 7. position dressed with Zodiac brand Oil.

Psalm to be read: Psalm of David No. 71.

Devotions: 30 minutes daily for nine days.

Similarly I learned that if it is desired to bring confusion *to the one who has caused* the unfavorable vibrations the opposite procedure should be followed. (See Fig. 5)

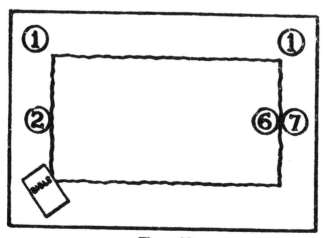

Fig. 5

Two White Candles (preferably of the shape of a crucifix) No. 1-1 position dressed with Hi-Altar Brand Oil.

*One Astral Candle in No. 2 position dressed with Zodiac
Brand Oil.*

*One Orange Candle in No. 6 position dressed with CON-
FUSION brand Oil.*

*One Black Candle in No. 7 position dressed with Con-
fusion brand Oil.*

Psalm to be read: Psalm 70.

Devotions: 30 minutes each evening before retiring.

> The Black candle only *should be extinguished*
> after reading the seventieth Psalm only *once.*

I also learned that for those who would rid themselves of all enemies the same procedure has been used
as described directly above except in the matter of
Psalm to be read: Psalm No. 59

Devotions: 30 minutes daily each evening before retiring. The black candle is extinguished after
reading the 59th Psalm *twice.*

Note: Compare this with Exercise 2 described and illustrated in **Chapter XIV.**

CHAPTER IX

THE USE of SYMBOL CANDLES

The use of so-called SYMBOL candles is a form of
Fire Worship which is strictly an American custom. How
it originated and where, no one seems to know.

That the use of SYMBOL candles has been prevalent in certain of our Southern States is well known and
the custom has gradually spread until forms of this
method of Candle Burning are found in many places including New York, Philadelphia, Chicago, Detroit, Pitts-
burgh, St. Louis and many cities and towns between.

A SYMBOLIC CANDLE is a vegetable oil or paraffin candle which is moulded in the shape of an animal — such as a cat or lion — or in the form of a human being. These candles are burned because, it is claimed, the symbolism involved is accentuated, crystalized.

In order to understand the symbolism involved as well as the rituals which are said to be used it is necessary to go to the Dark Continent.

Frazer and Blackman as well as many other accredited investigators have recorded many strange and weird rites of African Medicine Men. Some of the accomplishments of these individuals have caused investigators to marvel and at the same time have defied every logical explanation by them.

For example, there is the story of the brutal Congo trader who drove his workers like slaves, treated them disgracefully, and beat them into an early grave.

The native workmen, unable to endure it longer, sent one of their number a hundred miles into the interior where there resided a powerful medicine man. To him the story was unfolded and a promise of a rich reward made for alleviating the distressing condition of the workers. The medicine man agreed to help so when the emissary left the next day he carried with him a small package which he guarded carefully.

Having arrived back at his employer's plantation he gathered his fellow members about him and displayed the contents of the package — a small figure in human form made of clay with a thong of rawhide about its neck.

That evening when the trader was about to retire he noticed the idol upon his dresser. How it got there no one seemed to know. Calling one of his servants he made inquiries but the trembling servant was merely able to say that it portended evil — perhaps even death, by strangulation, to the trader.

This of course seemed ridiculous to the trader yet sensing discontent among his workers, he decided to keep armed at all times and to be wary. A week passed, then two, then three without any untoward incident. Always the idol stared blankly at him from his dresser from which he was determined not to remove it despite the fact that it caused him no end of annoyance and discomfort.

In the fourth week the trader came down with a fever which grew worse and worse. Finally in desperation he frantically called a servant and instructed him to fetch the nearest doctor.

When the doctor arrived he found the man — dead he had contracted pneumonia and choked to death.

This strange and terrible legend does not end here. In the course of events the story of the idol came out but the most minute investigation by the doctor could reveal nothing to disprove his first diagnosis. Strangely enough, the idol in question was still upon the dresser but THE HEAD HAD BEEN SNAPPED OFF!

The only explanation was that as the rawhide thong dried out it tightened more and more until it snapped off the head of the idol.

The use of symbolic idols of this kind is quite common in Africa. Many other tales of almost unbelievable happenings have been told by competent scientists who deal with facts.

In Dr. Haddon's Report on the Cambridge Anthropological Expedition to Torres Straits we find numerous instances of the use of SYMBOLS

It is quite common, for instance, for natives of this area to leave an idol or charm in the shape of a pregnant woman near the fire when they leave their homes for the day. The symbolism is self evident: Looking after the fire is woman's work and a woman in the condition represented would not be likely to leave the house and neglect the fire. Thus it is a SYMBOL of PROTECTION against all evil in the home.

Among other uses of idols which have been recorded is the custom of maidens who take a few strands of hair from their loved one and incorporate them into a small doll-like figure symbolic of the lover. A second doll-like figure contains a few hairs of the maiden and is symbolic of her.

These figures are placed facing each other at a distance from each other which is the exact height of the loved one. Each day the figures are moved closer to each other (a matter of an inch or two). It is believed that when the figures reach positions which are face to face or touching, the maiden shall have become a bride.

In a similar manner these natives practice a ritual exactly opposite to the above to drive away an unwelcome suitor, to rid one's self of a rival in love, to dispel an alleged suspected evil spirit or similar condition.

The foregoing seems a far call to the custom of SYMBOL CANDLE BURNING yet these particular customs have been related so that the analogy to modern candle burning rituals may become clear.

I must say, at this point, that this custom of SYMBOL CANDLE BURNING is not the highest, most devout, and purest expression of the Philosophy of Fire, but rather an off-shoot, a custom which has its origin in legend and natural tradition rather than in Revelation.

Figure 6

Nevertheless, there are many who are said to practice it and the following is based upon information gathered by the author from various sources including spiritual advisors, mediums, cultists, etc.

The most common use of SYMBOL CANDLES involves the use of candles which are moulded in human form. (See Fig. 6). Although they are avail-

able in various colors, a neutral tone (the color of pale coffee) is said to be the most desirable. A wick runs through the candle from top to bottom. It is so moulded that it will stand on its own feet without support.

In burning these candles the Altar is prepared much as has been described in Chapter VII but the diagrams which accompany the text will serve to clarify the explanation.

Let us take the hypothetical case of a young woman who desires to win the man of her dreams (or in the case of a man, the woman of his dreams). Two SYMBOL CANDLES are procured and dressed with Fire of Love Brand Oil.

The candles are then placed as shown in Fig 7

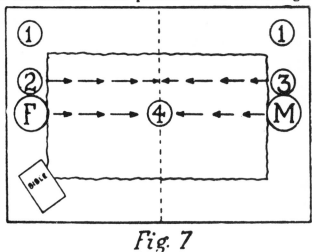

Fig. 7

In the Number 1-1 positions are **White** Crucifix Altar candles (dressed with Hi-Altar Brand Oil). In the 'F' position is the Symbol Candle symbolic of the woman (dressed with Fire of Love Brand Oil). In the 'M' position is the Symbol candle symbolic of the man (dressed with Fire of Love Brand Oil). In the No. 2 position is placed the ASTRAL candle of the woman (dressed with Zodiac Brand Oil). In the No. 3 position is placed the Astral candle of the man (Dressed with Zodiac brand Oil) In the No. 4 position is placed a RED candle or Fire of Love brand Candle (dressed with Crown of Success brand Oil or Fire of Love brand Oil).

Now note the symbolism involved in this arrangement. The White Crucifix Altar Candles denote purity and things of the Spirit.

The two Symbol Candles denote the man and woman involved.

The two Astral candles bring *personality* to the Symbol candles. Without them the **Symbol candles** would mean nothing. With the correct Astral candles, however, the Symbol Candles take on an added meaning for the vibrations of the Astral Candles give guiding light to the Symbol Candles.

In the No. 4 position is placed a RED candle which is symbolic of Love and Affection. In this case this is the Offeratory Candle.

When the candles are in the positions shown in the diagram all are lighted.

Then opening the Bible, Chapter 1 of the SONG of SOLOMON is read three times and all the candles extinguished except the red candle which is allowed to burn out.

The second day the *two* symbol candles are each moved two inches toward the center together with the Astral candles. (see direction of arrows in Fig. 7). Chapter 2 of the Song of Solomon is read. The new RED candle is allowed to burn out.

Each day a new RED candle is burned and the two Symbol candles and two Astral Candles are moved two inches closer to the center. Each day the succeeding Chapter of the Song of Solomon is read until all eight chapters have been read.

Ordinarily the Symbol Candles and the Astral Candles will last for the entire devotion since they are burned but a few minutes.

This devotion, it is stated, is practised by many devotees in many places. It should be borne in mind that the foregoing is purely a hypothetical case to show the ritualistic symbolism as devised by those who follow the Philosophy of Fire.

Let us take the hypothetical case of a young lady who is in love with a man who seems to be influenced by the affections of another young woman.

A candle burning ritual has been devised which is *symbolic of the dissolving of the attraction.*

In Figure 8 we see a different altar arrangement.

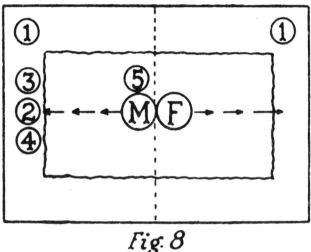

Fig. 8

In No. 1-1 positions are white Crucifix Altar Candles dressed with Hi-Altar brand Oil. In the "M" position is the symbol candle representing the man whose love is desired (dressed with Fire of Love brand Oil).

In the 5 position is the Man's Astral Candle dressed with Zodiac Oil. In the "F" position is the Symbol Candle representing the woman who *now has* the man's love. (dressed with Confusion brand Oil). Note that there is no guiding light of an Astral candle for this Symbol Candle. In the No. 2 position is a WHITE Candle dressed with Glow of Attraction brand Oil. This candle symbolizes Purity and the pure love which the young woman has for the man. In the No. 3 position is the young woman's Astral Candle (dressed with Zodiac brand Oil). In the No. 4 position is a RED or Fire of Love Brand candle (dressed with Fire of Love brand Oil) which symbolizes love.

The ritual is as follows: Candle "F" and "M" are placed *back to back at the center* and moved two inches *away* from each other each day. Each day a chapter of the Song of Solomon is read with *all* candles burning. Then all are extinguished except Number 1, 2, 3, 4, and are allowed to burn out. This is repeated until the eight chapters of the Song of Solmon are read. It will be seen that in this devotion the "M" candle is brought closer and closer to the No. 2 candle and *away* from the "F" candle.

The symbolic beauty of both the devotions described above cannot fail to impress the reader with its significance. Neither will the similarity to the African symbol worship be lost upon the reader. How the custom came to be revived in the form of Fire Worship cannot be explained but devotions similar to the hypothetical cases described above are said to be common in many sections.

CHAPTER X

CANDLE BURNING DURING TIME OF WAR

A DEEPLY SIGNIFICANT CUSTOM

Although war is perhaps the most ungod-like expression of the human race and is, in itself, an irreligious activity, yet it perhaps strengthens the religious instincts of man more than any other universal activity

Perhaps fear is the underlying reason for such an expression of religion during Time of War.

There are few families that are not touched by it. Sons, husbands, brothers and sweethearts are called to arms and the mothers, wives, sisters and loved ones left behind fear for the safety of those departed.

In normal times; in times of peace, women come to depend upon the strength and leadership of their menfolk. They look to them to make decisions; to provide for the home; to maintain order and happiness in the home. In short he is King to his Queen in the Kingdom of his Home.

When a man is called to war there is a definite let down. Confidence is undermined; fear tries to force its way into a woman's heart; Confusion reigns in one's mind; one cannot think clearly.

In such a condition it is only natural that those who are left at home should turn their faces heavenward seeking the Light Of Understanding and Strength; seeking Solace and Comfort; seeking Calmness and Dynamic Power.

At such a time when things seem dark and hope appears to have forsaken one, we turn instinctively to God for spiritual aid· We express our silent wish to Him that our loved ones will be brought safely back . . . . that he will be protected from all bodily injury; that his spirit will not be broken and that we may keep our own self-faith until that happy reunion.

Those who follow the Philosophy of Fire have studied the problems surrounding these circumstances and have delved deep into historical archives to rediscover for themselves and put to new use many of the half forgotten practices of the Ancient Zoroastrians.

It is known, of course, that the ancient Zoroastrians although a nominally peaceful people, did have their wars — whether wars were thrust upon them or whether they were wars of self-defense or in the attainment of some other objective.

Always, in such instances, the departing warrior did one of two things:

1) Built a fire upon the altar and prayed to the Holy Presence there to protect him from bodily harm and return him from the wars hale and whole. And in his prayer was included the thought that if the Divine Presence deemed it fitting to take his soul from its earthy home (his body) He would guide his spirit to Paradise where it would forever be engaged in the conflict with evil and the ultimate victory of Ahura-Mazda.

2) Occasionally, instead of merely praying, a sacrifice was made upon the Altar. Incense was burned and dedicated to the Deity. Sometimes he would offer up his sword and dedicate it to Ahura-Mazda in His fight to overcome Evil.

A fire thus lighted by a departing warrior was kept burning by his wife, his sons or daughters or his loved one. It was never allowed to go out. This vigil light was the symbol of his presence in the home and served to light the way for him spiritually during the dark days ahead. Only upon his return was the fire extinguished.

Present day followers of the Philosophy of Fire can adapt this beautiful custom to meet the needs of modern times in a ritual which is both beautiful in its symbolism and a source of warmth and affection.

Not only can this ritual be practised in memory of those who are called to war but also by women whose men folk have to travel long distances from home or by women whose husbands or sweethearts have strayed away and whose affection it is desired to retain.

This Memorial Ritual with all its deeply religious significance and symbolic beauty may be practised as follows:

The Altar is prepared with two, WHITE Crucifix Altar Candles in the No. 1-1 positions.

In the No. 2 position (which is the center) is placed a GIANT EVERLASTING TYPE CANDLE.

This type of candle is approximately 18" in height and when burned 15 minutes a day can be burned for about 200 days. They weigh two to three pounds each.

An even larger candle is available which weighs 13 pounds and burns for TWO YEARS when burned 3 or 4 hours daily. However, the smaller of the two mentioned is perfectly satisfactory for the present ritual.

This giant Candle should be a LIGHT BLUE COLOR which reference to Table No. II, shows is symbolic of "Spiritual Understanding, Soothing Happiness, Cool, Calm, Collected Thoughts; the Power to Perceive; PROTECTION"!

The diagram of the Altar would then be as shown in the following figure:

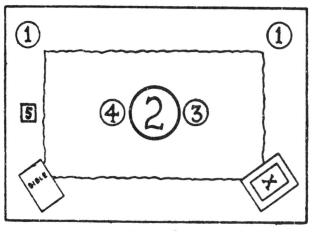

Fig. 9

No. 1-1 *positions WHITE Crucifix Altar candles dressed with Altar brand Oil.*

No. 2 *position GIANT candle (Light BLUE) dressed with CONQUERING Glory brand Oil.*

No. 3 and 4 positions — ASTRAL candle of the departing soldier dressed with Zodiac Brand Oil.

NOTE: The Bible is in the position indicated and, if available, a photograph of the departing soldier is placed as shown at "X".

The Ritual in this devotion may take any of several different forms but it would be a long remembered occasion if the following were adhered to:

The departing soldier gathers together with his family and loved ones and'after lighting the two No. 1-1 candles. the Bible is opened to Psalm 35 and the following verses are read either by the soldier or *by some one whom he designates.*

P S A L M   3 5

A Psalm of David

Pleading cause, O LORD, with them that strive with me: fight against them that fight against me.

2. Take hold of shield and buckler, and stand up for mine help.

3. Draw out also the spear, and stop the way against them that persecute me: say unto my soul, I am thy salvation.

4. Let them be confounded and put to shame that seek after my soul: let them be turned back and brought to confusion that devise my hurt.

5. Let them be as chaff before the wind: and let the angel of the LORD chase them.

6. Let their way be dark and slippery; and let the angel of the LORD persecute them.

7. For without cause they have hid for me their net in a pit, which without cause they have digged for my soul.

8. Let destruction come upon him at unawares: and let his net that he hath hid catch himself: into that very destruction let him fall.

9. And my soul shall be joyful in the LORD: it shall rejoice in his salvation.

* * *

19. Let not them that are mine enemies wrongfully rejoice over me, neither let them wink with the eye that hate me without cause.

20. For they speak not peace; but they devise deceitful matters against them that are quiet in the land.

When the foregoing verses from the 35th Psalm have been read the soldier then lights his ASTRAL candles and solemnly designates one of his loved ones to keep the candles burning while he is away.

Then those who are assembled kneel in silent prayer and meditation for a safe return (a full three minutes)

The Altar lights are then extinguished and the Astral lights are extinguished but the Giant BLUE candle is permitted to burn for (15 minutes). This ends the Ritual EXCEPT that each day some one must repeat the ritual in the following manner and order.

a. Light Altar Lights (No. 1-1)

b. Light GIANT BLUE Candle (No. 2)

c. Light Astral Candles (No. 3 and 4)

d. Read: PSALM 133 which follows:
Behold how good and how pleasant it is for brethren to dwell together in unity!

2. It is like the precious ointment upon the head that ran down upon the beard, even Aaron's beard; that went down to the skirts of his garments.

3. As the dew of Hermon, and as the dew that descended upon the mountains of Zion: for there the LORD commanded the blessing, even life forever more.

Extinguish altar lights (1-1)

f. Extinguish Astral lights (No. 3 and 4)

g. Allow GIANT BLUE candle (No. 2) to burn 15 minutes.

This exercise can be repeated each day while the soldier is away.

Now it may happen that the *soldier has already departed* and his loved ones at home desire to practice this ritual in his honor. The devotion can be followed as described here except that some one must *act for the departed soldier*, lighting the candles and reading the verses from the 35th Psalm and then extinguishing them just as described. This is called RITUAL BY PROXY.

After all, the symbolism, the beautiful sentiment involved, the deep seated devotion, the loving significance of the ritual is what really counts.

Those who have read the preceding chapters of this volume will immediately recognize the symbolism and the deeply religious significance of this Ritual.

It should be noted that this custom differs from the ancient practice of keeping the Altar Fire burning *at all times*. In the modern ritual, the candle is burned but 3 hours and then extinguished until the next day. However, the SAME CANDLES SHOULD BE USED from day to day. Since such a candle can be used for about 500 days (or nearly 1 year) it is usually big enough to meet *longer than* 1½ years and the giant candle is almost entirely burned, then a new candle is procured to replace the burned out candle. It should be noted that when CHANGING CANDLES, whether it is the GIANT BLUE, or the Altar Candles or the Astral Candle, the old candles are lighted first and the NEW candles lighted *from the old ones.* Then the old candles are extiguished and discarded.

It was pointed out at the beginning of this chapter that a modification of this Ritual can be practiced by those whose husbands or loved ones are travelling away from home — or who have been overcome by some tantalizing vision of some happier hunting ground.

For those who wish to insure the safe and willing return of such, a Ritual similar to that described can be followed. The difference lies in the fact that the candles are different colors and one extra candle is used. Note the following (Refer to Fig. 9)

No. 1-1 positions 2 White Crucifix Altar candles dressed with Hi-Altar brand Oil.

No. 2 position: GIANT RED Candle symbolizing Love dressed with Fire of Love brand Oil.

No. 3 position: Astral candle of the departed, dressed with Zodiac Oil.

No. 5 Position: Astral candle of the deserted one dressed with Zodiac Oil.

Ritual:—When the candles are first lighted read the 36th Psalm then extinguish all candles except the Giant Red and the Astral candle (No. 5 position).

Burn Giant Red Candle 15 minutes daily.

The same procedure can be followed each day.

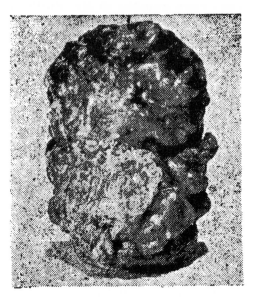

Hand-fixed VOTIVE Candles like this) are available in seven colors for each day of the week.

CHAPTER XI

WHAT EVERY FOLLOWER OF
THE PHILOSOPHY of FIRE SHOULD KNOW

The novitiate in the principles of the Philosophy of Fire will at first stumble upon many obstacles unless he or she first acquaints himself with certain fundamentals of the Art.

In the first place the Rituals, as practiced by so many, can be a delightful occasion, a deeply significant devotion, a truly soul-satisfying experience — or it can be a confused muddle, a hopeless waste of time.

In olden times candles used in the Philosophy of Fire Rituals were hand-made, of bees' wax or vegetable oil. They were colored with natural vegetable colors and moulded into symbolic shapes where required for certain devotions.

Dressing Oils were essences of certain flowers and no deviation was permitted.

However, it is now realized that some ancient customs cannot be practised today as they were centuries ago. They must be modified and adapted to meet the needs of individuals living in a fast moving world.

Again it should be repeated that it is the symbolism which counts as well as the sincerity and faith of the petitioner·

In ancient times the Zoroastrians could not go out to a corner store and purchase candles or incense and burner or altar cloth or candle stick holders or any of the other articles needed for their devotions. They had to fashion each article by hand.

Our great, great grandparents used to spin the wool from which they made the clothes they wore. Would it not be foolish for us to do this today when we can go into a store and buy ready made cloth and clothing which wears better, looks better, fits better and costs less?

The same applies to modern altar supplies for those who follow the Philosophy of Fire.

Candles, Candle sticks, Altar Cloths, Dressing Oils, Bibles, Incense and Incense Burners are available from reliable Supply Houses which are adequate for the purposes intended and far better in quality than the ancients ever dreamed of having.

There are some devotees of the Art who purchase unbranded candles in the particular colors they desire

to have.   They select the particular shade wanted and
dress them themselves with the particular Oil that they
wish to use.

On the other hand certain firms sell Branded Candles in pre-selected colors based upon Color Charts,
Symbolic Charts and Astral Charts similar to Table I
and Table II in another section of this volume·   Some
of these Branded Candles are listed as follows:

> SPARK of SUSPICION brand Candle (Brown)
> Yellow)
>
> FLAMING POWER brand Candle (White)
>
> ALTAR brand Candle (White)
>
> FIRE of LOVE brand Candle (Red)
>
> FIERY WALL of PROTECTION brand Candle (Light
> Blue)
>
> RADIANT HEALTH brand Candle (Red)
>
> PROSPERITY brand Candle (Light Green)
>
> WEALTHY WAY brand Candle (Green)
>
> GLOW of ATTRACTION brand Candle (Gold or
> Yellow)
>
> INFLAMMATORY CONFUSION brand Candle (Dark
> Blue)
>
> BENEFICIAL DREAM brand Candle (Lavendar)
>
> CROWN of SUCCESS brand Candle (Orange)
>
> PEACEFUL HOME brand Candle (Light Blue)
>
> SATAN-BE-GONE brand Candle (Orchid)
>
> CRUCIBLE of COURAGE brand Candle (Orange)
>
> CONQUERING GLORY brand Candle (Purple)
>
> LADY LUCK brand Candle (Gold)
>
> WEED of MISFORTUNE brand Candle (Black)

In addition to the above mentioned Brands of Candles there are 12 ASTRAL Candles each Branded and

in colors to correspond to the various Signs of the Zodiac Reference to Table I in Chapter V will enable you to select the proper Astral Candle When you order from your dealer always give your date of birth and let him select your Astral Candle for you or in the case of branded candles, note the tag or band upon it. Usually you will find the Sign of the Zodiac, the month and other descriptive information. With such branded candles you just cannot go wrong.

The size of candle to use is a matter which is largely dependent upon the individual choice but my choice would be a 11 inch candle because experience has shown that there is less waste and therefore it is most economical in the long run. Astral candles usually come about 10 inches high, should preferably be of the HAND FIXED type and about 1-¾ inches in diameter.

The only candles which should be REUSED from one Ritual to another are the ALTAR candles and the AS TRAL candles of the petitioner· *All other candles should be discarded and not reused after the ritual* unless the same ritual is continued from day to day or from time to time. Many people start each *new* ritual for each *new* purpose with an entirely *new set* of candles and this truly is the most logical procedure to follow for it insures an altar of outstanding beauty and dignity.

The reason for this procedure is perfectly obvious. For instance, a Fiery Wall of Protection Brand Candle is a LIGHT BLUE Candle while a PEACEFUL HOME Brand Candle is also of a LIGHT BLUE color. However, these candles usually would be dressed with a different oil and if a Blue used candle which had been dressed with a particular oil were re used later for another purpose *the symbolism would be lost* because of the improper dressing.

This is not true of Altar type candles which are always dressed with Hi-Altar type Oil or Astral Candles which are always dressed with Zodiac type Oil Thus, these *may* be re-used.

In the matter of Dressing Oils, these may be selected by Brand Name also. Usually if you order a particular candle or candles, your dealer will be able to tell you the proper dressing oil to use as he will be guided by your seection of the candle. Some Supply Houses sell each candle with its accompanying Dressing Oil, but this is not practical or economical except in the Case of ASTRAL Candles where one Ziodiac Bran.! Dressing Oil serves for all Signs of the Zodiac.

My suggestion to a beginner would be to purchase one of the Basic Candle Burning Kits such as are available today. A Kit of this kind includes a dozen or more small bottles of various dressing oils and two large sized bottles of Altar type and Zodiac type oils. There are also a pair of Crucifix shaped White Altar Candles and an Astral Candle for the purchaser's own Sign. A kit like this saves you money in the first place *and* it gives you a complete supply of dressing oils so that you can practice any ritual you desire *when you want to* There is never any need to wait until you order them. After all, the best time to burn candles is when you are spiritually inspired and in the proper mood.

The same Supply House from whom you purchase your candles can supply you with incense, incense burners. candle sticks and other supplies.

Symbol candles are sometimes difficult to obtain but are available from reliable Supply Houses who really serve the needs of followers of the Philosophy of Fire

PERVERTED SYMBOLISM

or

BLACK ART in CANDLE BURNING

Every cause has its effect. Each movement, each action, every thought sets in motion factors which enter into eternal conflict, one with the other.

The blackness of night offsets the light of day; the cold of winter balances the warmth of summer sun; there are the forces of evil to upset the forces of good; there is Heaven and hell; good people and bad!

And this Law of Balance has touched the noble custom of Candle Burning, too. We cannot say that it has greatly affected those who follow the Philosophy of Fire because their thoughts and hearts and mind are on too lofty a plane to be thus polluted.

During the Dark Ages in Europe when culture was almost a lost art; when morals and ethics and religion were at their lowest ebb; when Satanism ruled the hearts and minds of men, there were certain cults of mad adventurers who attempted to rule the people by using religion as a whip.

In those days religion was highly symbolic; it was bread and wine to the multitude and was the only thing to which the common man could turn for comfort and solace.

Recognizing the almost fanatical zeal with which the peasant classes clung to their religion these religious racketeers used the church as an instrument to gain their desires. Fantastic superstitions were hatched; witches grew powerful; the churches were subdued. Gradually these early racketeers changed rituals, perverted the devotional exercises to such an extent that the infamous Black Mass was practised.

One thing these racketeers *did* leave. That was the wealth of SYMBOLISM which was so much a part of the early Roman Church. However, the symbolism was changed. Instead of symbolising the goodness, the beauty, the divine forces, each passage of the mass was debased by symbolising all the forces of degraded nature and base hideousness.

Even today the forces of evil are smouldering in the for most of us, however, the forces of good are too strong to permit evil to make too much progress.

There are some individuals who, having studied the symbolism involved in the Philosophy of Fire, have adapted the rituals to serve their personal whims and desires rather than the common cause of Good.

Although this volume is not intended to delve too deeply into this phase of Fire Worship, it is nevertheless a wise precaution on the part of the novitiate interested in the Philosophy of Fire to know *both sides* of the picture.

Those who practice this form of Fire Worship retain the SYMBOLISM of the Philosophy of Fire but the basic SYMBOLISM is INVERTED.

For example we have seen in previous chapters how followers of the Philosophy of Fire dress their Altars with WHITE ALTAR CANDLES as a symbol of Purity, Chastity, Spiritual Elevation, Truth and Justice. White symbolizes all these things. It is only fitting that white be used to be inviting to the Divine presence at the Altar.

In the debased form of Fire Worship (sometimes referred to as Black Ritual) BLACK ALTAR CANDLES are used to dress the Altar since this color symbolizes the *opposite* of white or the forces of iniquity.

Whereas in True Fire Worship bright colored candles are used — and in the lighter shades, in Black Ritual dark shades are used. For example, muddy brown-green, greenish yellow, purple red, very dark brown, midnight blue, black, etc.

In order to get a true perspective of Black Ritual it is again necessary to go back into historical records to seek out origins, to investigate customs and practices which are analagous to those practiced today in Black Ritual. It is only by doing this that we can truly understand the symbolism involved.

Many volumes have been written on the subject of Black Art, Necromancy, Black Magic, Voodooism and other similar occult practices and it is not our purpose to deal with them here. It should be noted, however, that all such Magic is based on the Law of Sympathy.

This means that *like* attracts *like*· Things in relation to another always bear the same relation. Unlike things repel unlike things.

Does not a child bear some of the characteristics of its mother and its father —no matter how far that child may be removed?

Sympathetic Magic was practiced by the Ojebway Indians, for example. When a member of this tribe wished to work evil on anyone, he fashioned an image in the likeness of his enemy and then either shot an arrow through the image or ran a needle through his head or where the heart would be located in reality.

It was thought that wheresoever the needle ran its course or where the arrow pierced the image, the enemy would be seized with a sharp pain in a corresponding place in his body.

In the Malayan Peninsula a similar custom has been described by archaeologists and explorers. There the native who has an enemy seeks to get a few hairs from his enemy as well as nail parings, a piece of his garment, or any personal effect of the enemy in question.

These items are then mixed with wax from a deserted bee's comb and molded into an image in human form. This is thought to symbolize the enemy. Naturally such a charm is supposed to bring one into contact with the subject of his hate.

The Malayan then builds a fire and after placing the image on a spit, turns it over and over until the image has melted away. This is thought to dispel any charm or crossed condition which the enemy may hold over one.

History has recorded many similar beliefs and customs. For example, the belief is prevalent in many countries of the world, including our own, that if a hunter drives a nail into the foot-print of an animal, it will be easy for the hunter to catch him.

Similarly there is the belief that if a nail is driven into the foot-print of one's enemy it will lame him (symbolically) or cripple his efforts to cause harm.

The author recalls a story which was related to him by a Canadian farmer living in the Province of Quebec.

This man lived a number of miles from town, which was reached by a dirt highway winding twelve miles around the mountains or by a foot path which took a short cut through the woods a distance of only four miles.

Usually the trip to town was made on foot because of the shorter distance and the time saved. It was necessary, however, to traverse the property of a neighboring farmer who was his bitter enemy.

It happened that the neighbor had warned this farmer of dire consequences in the event he trespassed his property but one day, heedless of the warning, the farmer took the foot path to town. He had gone a considerable distance and was at about the middle of his neighbor's property when he was suddenly taken with a seizure of paralysis. He could lift neither his left foot nor his right foot — try as he might. Both feet seemed glued to the ground.

When his first spasm of fright had passed he began to take stock of his predicament· Then he perceived his unfriendly neighbor approaching with a smirk upon his face.

It was then that he learned the terrible secret. His neighbor stated that he had "put a curse" upon the farmer and that he could not walk until he, the neighbor, so willed it or until he had removed a nail which he had driven into the foot prints the farmer had left behind.

Upon questioning, the neighbor admitted that the "curse" would be ineffective at any point except when trespassing upon his property. Thereupon he made off leaving the farmer to stay through the cold autumn night.

This story was of particular interest to me because it was analagous to similar beliefs which have been prevalent in many widely separated countries.

But back to the hero of this amazing adventure. The manner of his release from his predicament is no less astounding than his sudden seizure and the symbolism involved in his escape is no less startling than that of his "psychic paralysis".

As he stood there in the cold autumn twilight he tried to remember everything he had ever heard of natural magic, of phenomena of this sort, of the symbolism involved·

He realized that his enemy had driven a nail in his foot print to cause paralysis. He realized, too, that he was trespassing on another's property. He realized his wrong. Then he saw a solution.

Stripping off his coat he ripped it apart and with great difficulty he managed to force a part of it under one of his feet. Immediately his foot was free. He then freed the other foot in a like manner.

Then wrapping the parts of his coat about his feet he began to walk off the property. Arrived at the edge of the field he found the nail in the path, pulled it up, removed the wrappings from his feet and found he was a free man once more.

It is interesting to note that *symbolically* when his feet were wrapped in his coat he was then *WALKING ON HIS OWN PROPERTY* and thus not affected by the "spell" which had been cast upon him.

This story, as incredulous as it may sound, is true, so this Canadian farmer says, and no amount of cross-examination could change his story one iota. Perhaps this story falls into the same category as many which have been related by scientists on their return from Darkest Africa; baffling to them, unexplained and unexplainable. Who knows?

Now the foregoing story as well as the various practices described have been given for a purpose — to show the *motives* behind the Black Arts and the Black Rituals which some people attempt to practice.

These practices clearly indicate that the rituals involved were not of high ethical or moral value. They had in them the essence of evil. It is true that in some of them the evil was not great. No great harm came of the practices themselves yet it cannot be imagined for a moment that the rituals were practiced to gain some high spiritual value.

Now let us see in what manner the symbolism we have already discussed has been adapted by some people who today use Fire Worship in the hope of securing some similar manifestation regardless of consequences.

Spiritual advisors, mediums, clairvoyants and other investigators of religious ethics are familiar with many of such practices from personal experience as they are usually the object of many a confidence.

I will relate the episode of the man who stated that from time to time he was missing certain things of a most personal nature. He noted that a circular hole had been cut from the palm of his left hand glove; that a "V" shaped clipping had been taken from the tail of his shirt; that the toe end of his sock had been clipped off; that his tooth brush had been stolen; that his comb had turned up after a day or so, but that the residue had been removed from between its teeth; a hole appeared mysteriously in his trouser pockets, cleanly cut with a scissors.

These mysterious happenings occurred over a period of weeks and coincident with these, Dame Fortune seemed to frown upon his every activity. Bad luck hounded him; he suffered from nerves, loss of appetite, lack of sleep.

It was only then that he learned that a rival had taken the things in question in order to place him in a "Crossed Condition".

He felt his condition so acutely that he sought comfort in the Philosophy of Fire. Unfortunately he was advised by a devotee who used Black Ritual instead of White and the practice was approximately as follows:

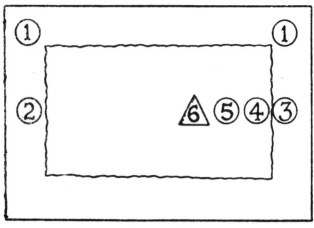

Fig. 10

Position 1-1 *Black Altar Candles dressed with Uncrossing brand Oil.*

Position 2 *His Astral Candle dressed with Zodiac brand Oil.*

Position 3 *Astral Candle of Rival dressed with Zodiac brand Oil.*

Position 4 *Midnight Blue — Inflammatory Confusion brand Candle dressed with Inflammatory Confusion brand Oil.*

Position 5 *Light Blue Fiery Wall of Protection brand Candle dressed with Protection brand Oil.*

NOTE: *Some devotees of the Art prefer the Blue GUARDIAN SYMBOL Candle instead of the regulation blue protective-type Candle. This Candle is molded to resemble a human figure in long flowing robes, similar to those worn by ancient priests, etc*

Position 6   *In this position was placed a clipped piece of sock, glove, shirt, hair, tooth brush bristles and other items identical with those taken by the rival. All were placed in an incense burner or similar receptacle. (See Fig. 10 above).*

Ritual: First the No. 2 candle is lit; then the No. 5 candle, then No. 4 candle then No. 3 candle. Last the No. 1-1 candles are lit.

When all candles are lighted the Bible is opened and the 53rd Psalm is read. Then the No. 1-1 candles are extinguished. The others are burned until consumed.

Second day repeat the first day but read PSALM 25.

Third day repeat first day but read PSALM 23. After reading the 23rd Psalm on the 3rd day the contents of the incense burner No. 8 should be burned by lighting it from Candle No. 2.

The symbolism here is explained as follows: Black Altar Candles are used because an evil influence dominates the scene. The worshipper is not indulging in a strictly evil practice but neither are the conditions free from contamination.

The Confusion type Candle and the Protection type Candle in the 4 and 5 positions serve to subdue or dominate the light from the rival's Astral Candle in 3 position. Thus, symbolically the contents of the receptacle 6 are UNAFFECTED by any influences except the worshipper's own Astral vibrations. In the symbolism employed, this may be interpreted as making the worshipper the Master of his own Destiny.

The Black candles are burned for a short time only because they are said to give off depressing vibrations and should be used sparingly.

A ritual of this kind is thought to dispel or relieve any "crossed condition" and to reflect it back into the face of him who has caused the unfavorable vibrations.

The writer gives the following ritual which has been used to symbolically "BRING CONFUSION OR TO EXERT PRESSURE ON ONE'S ENEMIES".

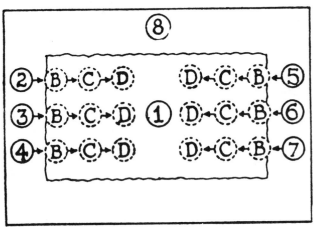

Fig. 11

No. 1 *position   The Astral Candle of the enemy dressed with Zodiac brand Oil.*

No. 2, 3, 4 *positions   Black Altar Candles dressed with Inflammatory Confusion brand Oil.*

No. 5, 6, 7, *positions   Midnight Blue Inflammatory Confusion brand Candles dressed with Inflammatory Confusion brand Oil*

No. 8 *position   Astral Candle of the subject dressed with Zodiac brand Oil and Domination brand Oil.*

Ritual: First light No. 8 candle
           Second light 5, 6, 7 candles
           Third light 2, 3, 4 candles
           Fourth light No. 1 candle

Read: — PSALM No. 3
           Allow all candles to burn 30 minutes then put
           them out. Candle 8 should be put out last

Second day: Move candles 2, 3, 4 to 2B 3B 4B
           Move candles 5, 6, 7 to 5B 6B 7B
           Repeat ritual of first day

Third day and Fourth Day:
           Move candles closer to the center each day
           Repeat ritual of first day

Explanation of the symbolism involved: Since the No. 1 candle is the Astral candle of the enemy this symbolizes that person. The three black Candles symbolize the unfavorable aspects the subject wishes to bring to bear against the enemy. The three midnight blue candles symbolize the confused state of mind or unfavorable vibrations which the subject wishes to bring against the enemy.

When these candles are moved closer each day for three consecutive days it symbolizes a bringing of pressure and an approaching consummation of the objective.

It will be noted that No. 8 candle which is the Astral Candle of the subject is far back on the Altar and thus is not influenced in any way by the black and blue candles.

Symbolically, this is a very strong ritual for if one considers the potential power of the vibrations which are given off, as calculated by those who follow the Philosophy of Fire, it would be dangerous (symbolically) except when used by one well conversant in the art, according to those who claim to know of such things.

Here is another Black Ritual. This one is used
**WHEN TWO ARE IN LOVE WITH THE SAME PER-
SON AND THE STUDENT WISHES TO ELIMINATE
THE RIVAL.**

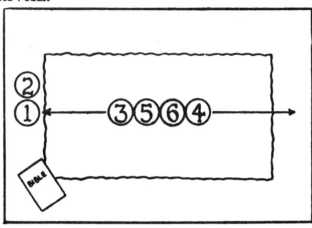

Fig. 12

No. 1 *Astral Candle of the subject dressed with Zodiac
brand Oil.*

No. 2 *Glow of Attraction brand Candle dressed with
Glow of Attraction brand Oil.*

No. 3 *Astral Candle of the Loved one dressed with
Zodiac brand Oil.*

No. 4. *Astral Candle of the Rival — dressed with Zodiac
brand Oil.*

No. 5 *Fiery Wall of Protection brand Candle (or Blue
Symbol Guardian Candle) dressed with Fiery
Wall of Protection brand Oil.*

No..6 *Midnight Blue Inflammatory Confusion brand
Candle dressed with Inflammatory brand Oil.*

Ritual: Light candles in this order 1, 2, 3, 4, 5, 6

Read   Song of Solomon Chapter 1

Each day candles No. 3 and 4 are moved two inches away from the center (see arrows) until No.

3 arrives directly in front of No. 1. All lights are extinguished immediately after reading the Biblical passage noted.

Explanation of the symbolism involved: It will be noted that a Confusion type Candle is placed directly alongside the Astral Candle of the rival so that its vibrations may affect the Astral Candle of the rival. However, the Protection type Candle affords protection for the Astral Candle of the loved one against any unfavorable vibrations from the rival's candle or the Confusion brand candle. The Astral candle of the subject (No. 1) with its accompanying Attraction type Candle (No. 2) affords a favorable combination of vibrations, symbolically speaking.

This same ritual is said to be used when two people are after the same job and the subject wishes to burn offeratory candles for this purpose. The only difference is that a Green Crown of Success brand Candle dressed with Crown of Success brand Oil is used instead of the Glow of Attraction brand Candle in the No. 2 position.

To be read: The 93rd Psalm

CHAPTER XIII

RULES TO FOLLOW IN ART of CANDLE BURNING

In the foregoing chapters your author has related numerous legends and customs and described practices which have been uncovered by anthropologists and historians in various parts of the world.

In each case where a ritual of candle burning was described, your author has dug deeply into the records to find an analogy; to seek the origin of the symbolism involved. This has been done to make it clear that in any form of worship "everything new in it is old and everything old in it is new".

It is to be hoped that the rituals and exercises which have been described up to this point are clearly understood and that the all-important symbolism involved has been understood as well.

If you have read well. you have learned certain fundamental rules which are recognized by those who follow the Philosophy of Fire. Review them again:

1. Each color has its own vibration and is said to give off a "vibratory influence".

2. Color of a candle is determined by the desired objective of the one who burns the candle, and is chosen in accordance with generally accepted "harmony" tables (see Chapter V.)

3. A candle may be used to symbolize any individual *providing* it is accompanied by or is, itself, the Astral Candle of that individual.

4. The Astral Candle of an individual is determined by the date of birth of that individual (see Table I, Chapter V.)

5. *Movement* toward or away, for or against an individual or object or desire may be symbolized by the progressive or successive stages or positions in which the symbolic candles are placed by the burner.

6. Candles should be dressed with oil (animal fat excepted) of a corresponding or harmonious vibratory color and influence.

7. Candles when once used in one specific ritual should NOT be used in a new ritual for a different intention even though the left-over candles may have

been only partially used. However, it is perfectly alright to use partially burned candles from day to day IF THE RITUAL IS *CONTINUED* FROM DAY TO DAY. The only exception to this is the use of ALTAR type candles and ASTRAL type candles of the petitioner. These *may* be used from one ritual to another but it is *preferable* to start each new ritual with a complete set of new candles.

These seven fundamental rules are simple and easy to follow and if they are well remembered anyone may recognize the symbolism involved in any candle burning exercise or ritual. By adhering to these basic fundamentals. the more progressive individual may create his own particular symbolism, rituals and exercises to satiate his own thirst for spiritual development and satisfaction.

Those readers desirous of practicing the exercises described in this volume are urged to exert care in the selection of Candles of known quality for they should *not* contain animal fats of any kind. Care should also be exercised in the selection of just the right color of candle.

All the brands of candles mentioned in this book were named because of their uniformly high quality, because they were free of animal fats and because they enjoy a wide sale among reliable Supply Houses.

The exercises in the following chapters are practised by various followers of the Philosophy of Fire. No supernatural claims whatsoever are made in connection with these exercises. The objectives of these exercises, as indicated by the titles, are merely the symbolic representations of the innermost desires of the original devotees who create them for the satisfaction of their own inhibitions. In each case the following information is given:

1. Intention of the exercise
2. Diagram illustrating manner of dressing Altar
3. Color of candles used
4. Size and type of candles (if other than usual size and shape)
5. Dressing oil used
6. Movement of candles (if any)
7. Suggested Biblical reading or Psalm
8. Suggested number of days for exercise

It is to be hoped that those interested in this ancient art will gain new insight into so noble a custom which has been perpetuated by those who follow the Philosophy of Fire.

CHAPTER XIV

SUGGESTED EXERCISES

EXERCISE 1

TO SETTLE A DISTURBED CONDITION IN THE HOME

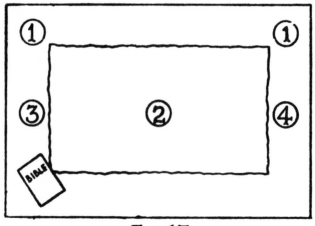

Fig. 13

Position 1-1 *White Crucifix type Altar Candles dressed with Hi-Altar brand Oil.*

Position 2 *GIANT TYPE 500-hour burning type light blue Candle (of a Peaceful Home brand or similar type) dressed with Crown of Success brand Oil* *

Position 3 *Astral Candle of Petitioner dressed with Zodiac brand Oil*

Position 4 *Pink Candle (or Happiness brand Candle) dressed with Crown of Success brand Oil.*

NOTE: If desired a Red Candle (or Fire of Love brand Candle) may be placed alongside the No. 4 candle dressed with Fire of Love brand Oil.

Suggested Bible Reading: First Psalm.

Devotions: Light candles in this order 1-1, 2, 3, 4. The GIANT 500-hour type candle* should be allowed to burn continuously until it is burned out. The other candles are lighted only 15 minutes a day while the First Psalm is read and re-read during the 15 minute period.

*If desired an A Peaceful Home Brand VOTIVE type candle may be used. In this case 1 candle is burned each day.

of followers of the Philosophy of Fire.

EXERCISE 2

TO OVERCOME AN ENEMY

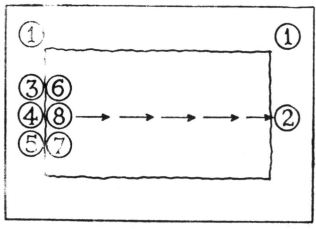

Fig. 14

Position 1-1   *White Crucifix type Altar Candles dressed with Hi-Altar brand Oil.*

Position 2   *Black Candle (or Weed of Misfortune brand Candle) dressed with Inflammatory Confusion brand Oil.*

Positions 3, 4, 5 *Three White Candles UNBRANDED to symbolize Purity (or Flaming Power brand Candles dressed with Power brand Oil).*

Positions 6 *and* 7 *Light Blue Candles (or Fiery Wall of Protection brand Candles*) dressed with Fiery Wall of Protection brand Oil.*

Position 8   *Dark Blue Candle (or Inflammatory Confusion brand Candle) dressed with Inflammatory Confusion brand Oil.*

MOVEMENT: Move candle 8 two inches daily in direction of arrows.

Suggested Bible Reading: Psalm 59.

Devotions: — Light No. 2 candle last. Read 59th Psalm then extinguish No. 2 candle. Allow other candles to burn 1 hour longer. Daily until satisfied.

If preferred the Blue GUARDIAN SYMBOL Candle may be used instead of regulation Fiery Wall of Protection brand Candles.

EXERCISE 3

TO OBTAIN MONEY

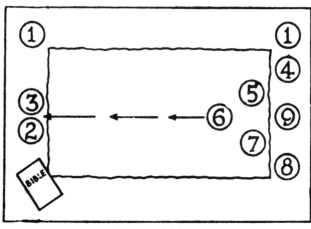

Fig. 15

Position 1-1 *White Crucifix Altar Candles dressed with Hi-Altar brand Oil.*

Position 2 *Astral Candle of the petitioner dressed with Zodiac Brand Oil.*

Position 3 *Gold Candle (or Glow of Attraction brand Candle) dressed with Glow of Attraction brand Oil.*

Positions 4, 5, 6, 7, 8 *Green Candles (Wealthy Way brand Candles) dressed with Lady Luck brand Oil.*

Position 9 *Garnet Candle (or Fiery Command brand Candle) dressed with Fiery Command brand Oil.*

MOVEMENT: Move candles 4 to 9 in direction of arrows two inches daily. Note that influence of candle 9 symbolically "drives" other candles toward objective.

Suggested Bible Reading: Psalm 41

Devotion: One hour each evening until satisfied.

EXERCISE 4

TO WIN THE LOVE OF MAN OR WOMAN

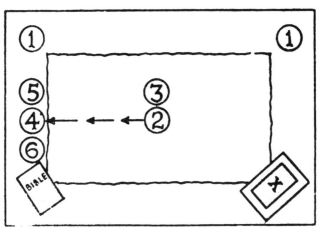

Fig. 16

Position 1-1 *WHITE Crucifix ALTAR candles dressed with Hi-Altar brand Oil.*

Position 2 *Red Candle (or Fire of Love brand Candle) dressed with Fire of Love brand Oil.*

Position 3 *Astral Candle of the one that is loved, dressed with Zodiac brand Oil.*

Position 4 *Red Candle (or Fire of Love brand Candle) dressed with Fire of Love brand Oil.*

Position 5 *Astral Candle of the one who seeks love dressed with Zodiac brand Oil.*

Position 6 *GOLD Candle (or Glow of Attraction brand Candle) dressed with Glow of Attraction brand Oil.*

NOTE:—The No. 6 Candle can be omitted if desired, but note the symbolism of this candle.
In position "X", may be placed a photo of the loved one if one is available.

MOVEMENT: Move No. 2 and 3 candles in direction of arrows 1 inch each day.

Suggested Bible Reading: If the candle burner is a *man* then read the Song of Solomon *Chapter 6.* If the candle burner is a *woman* read the Song of Solomon *Chapter 8.*

Devotions:—Burn candles two hours each day until satisfied.

NOTE:—A mixture of Frankincense and Myrrh may be burned while reading the Biblical passages referred to above. Place incense burner between Bible and Photo.

Large Crucifix Candles are economical. They come 9" high by 5" across, are long burning and in both black and white

EXERCISE 5

TO CONQUER FEAR

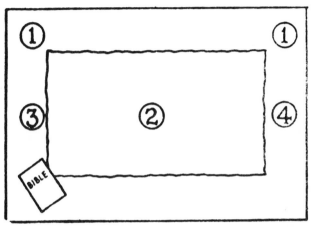

Fig. 17

Position 1-1 both *WHITE* Crucifix *ALTAR* Candles dressed with Hi-Altar brand Oil.

Position 2 Astral Candle of the Petitioner, dressed with Zodiac brand Oil.

Position 3 *O R A N G E* Candle (or *C r u c i b l e of* Courage brand Candle) dressed with Crucible of Courage brand Oil.

Position 4 *WHITE* Candle (or *Flaming Power brand* Candle) dressed with Flaming Power brand Oil.

Suggested Bible Reading: Psalm 31; in its entirety. Burn candles while reading. 5 minutes of meditation. Repeat for nine days or until satisfied

TO CHANGE ONE'S LUCK

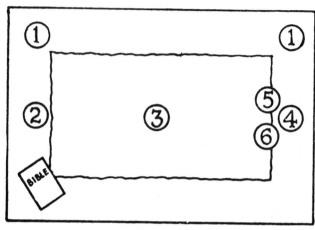

Fig. 18

Position 1-1 *White Crucifix Altar Candles dressed with Hi-Altar brand Oil.*

Position 2   *Astral Candle of the Petitioner dressed with Zodiac brand Oil.*

Position 3   *Light Blue Candle (or Fiery Wall of Protection brand Candle) dressed with Fiery Wall of Protection brand Oil.*

Position 4   *Black Candle (or Weed of Misfortune brand Candle) undressed.*

Positions 5 *and* 6 *Light Green Candles (or Prosperity brand Candles) dressed with Lady Luck brand Oil.*

Suggested Bible Reading: Psalm 62: verse 11

Devotions: Light candles in this order 1, 2, 3, 5, 6 and 4 *last*. Read the 11th verse of the 62nd Psalm three times and extinguish No. 4 only. After 15 minutes relight No. 4 candle read verse three times and extinguish No. 4 candle. Repeat this each 15 minutes for 1 hour and extinguish all candles. Repeat daily until satisfied. If preferred the Blue GUARDIAN symbol candle may be used instead of the regulation Fiery Wall of Protection brand Candle.

Two types of giant candles. The one on the left is 18" high and weighs 2 to 3 lbs. It burns at least 50 hours. The larger type is sometimes used but has not been found practical for general use.

TO GAIN POWER OVER OTHERS

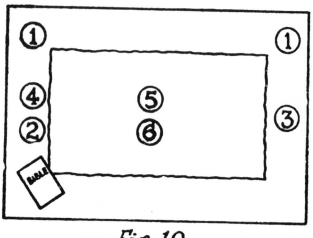

Fig. 19

Position 1-1 *Black Crucifix Altar Candles dressed with XX DOUBLE CROSS brand Oil.*

Position 2 *Astral Candle of petitioner dressed with Zodiac brand Oil.*

Position 3 *Astral Candle of person over whom power is sought dressed with Zodiac brand Oil.*

Position 4 *White Candle (or Flaming Power brand Candle) dressed with Power brand or Domination brand Oil.*

Position 5 *Purple Candle (or Conquering Glory brand Candle) dressed with Conquering Glory brand Oil.*

Position 6 *Orange Candle (or Crown of Success brand Candle) dressed with Crown of Success brand Oil.*

Movement: Move candles 5 and 6 toward candle 3 two inches each day.

Suggested Bible Reading: Psalm No. 130

Devotions 1 hour nightly for six days or longer if desired.

EXERCISE 8

TO AROUSE DISCORD, ANGER or JEALOUSY

IN ANOTHER

Fig. 20

Position 1-1 *Black Crucifix Altar Candles dressed with XX Double Cross brand Oil.*

Position 2 *Astral Candle of person who is object of wrath, dressed with Zodiac brand Oil.*

Position 3 *Brown Candle (or Spark of Suspicion brand Candle) dressed with Domination brand Oil.*

Position 4 *Black Candle (or Weed of Misfortune brand Candle) dressed with Inflammatory Confusion brand Oil*

Suggested Bible Reading: Psalm 70

Devotion   Each Monday and Friday for three weeks. **Burn candles 15 minutes at each devotion.**

TO GAIN PROSPERITY

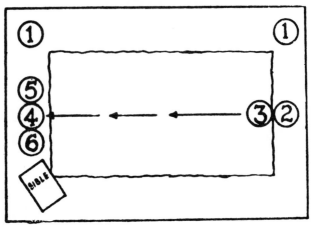

Fig. 21

(Note: The vibratory influences expressed symbolically by the colors suggested are thought to be particularly powerful)

Position 1-1 *White Crucifix Altar Candles dressed with Hi-Altar brand Oil.*

Position 2   *Light Green Candle (or Prosperity brand Candle (dressed with Crown of Success brand Oil.*

Position 3   *Gold Candle (or Glow of Attraction brand Candle) dressed with Glow of Attraction brand Oil.*

Position 4   *Astral Candle of the petitioner dressed with Zodiac brand Oil.*

Position 5   *Purple Candle (or Conquering Glory brand Candle) dressed with Glow of Attraction brand Oil.*

Position 6   *Orange Candle (or Crucible of Courage brand Candle) dressed with Glow of Attraction brand Oil.*

MOVEMENT: Candles 2 and 3 are moved in directions of arrows 2 inches each day.

Suggested Bible Reading: Psalm 41
Devotions: One hour daily until satisfied.

EXERCISE 10

TO PROTECT AGAINST EVIL INFLUENCES
FOR THOSE WHO ARE IN A SO-CALLED
"CROSSED CONDITION"

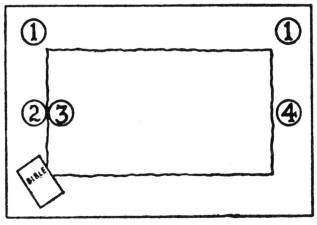

Fig. 22

Position 1-1 *White Crucifix Altar Candles dressed with Hi-Altar brand Oil.*

Position 2 *ORCHID Candle (or Satan-be-Gone brand Candle) dressed with Uncrossing brand Oil.*

Position 3 *ORANGE Candle (or Crown of Success brand Candle) dressed with Uncrossing brand Oil.*

Position 4 *Astral Candle of petitioner dressed with Zodiac brand Oil.*

Suggested Bible Reading Psalm of David No. 71
Devotions: 30 minutes daily for 9 days.

CHAPTER XV

MORE SUGGESTED EXERCISES

EXERCISE 11

TO WIN OR HOLD HAPPINESS

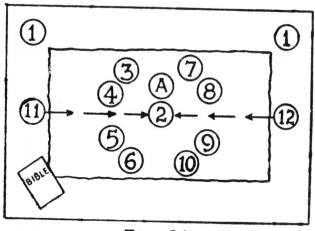

Fig 23

Position 1-1 *White Crucifix Altar Candles dressed with Hi-Altar brand Oil.*

Position 2 *Astral Candle of the petitioner dressed with Zodiac brand Oil.*

Positions 3 4, 5, 6 *Purple Candles (or Conquering Glory brand Candles) dressed with Conquering Glory brand Oil.*

Positions 7, 8, 9, 10 *Pink Candles (or Happiness brand Candles) dressed with Crown of Success brand Oil.*

Positions 11, 12 *Garnet Candles (or Fiery Command brand Candles) dressed with Crown of Success brand Oil.*

Disregard position "A" as this applies to Exercise 17 only
MOVEMENT: Move Candles 11 and 12 two inches daily in direction of arrows.

NOTE how Astral Candle is "cradled" by very strongly symbolic color vibrations.

Suggested Bible Reading: Psalm No. 11

Devotions: One hour each evening for 18 days or until satisfied.

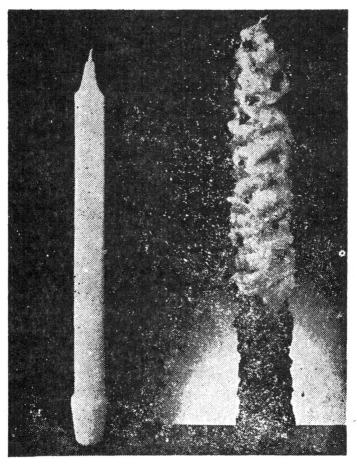

*LEFT: Recommended type Offeratory Candle, **10" or 11"** high. available in 14 colors Recommended quality usually has seal or brand name upon it. RIGHT: Astral candle of hand-fixed variety 10" high 1½" diameter. Note the two-color effect and speckles. available in authentic colors for each sign of Zodiac.*

EXERCISE 12

TO HEAL AN UNHAPPY MARRIAGE

Position 1-1   *White Crucifix Altar Candles dressed with Hi-Altar brand Oil.*

Position 2   *Astral Candle of husband dressed with Zodiac brand Oil.*

Position 3   *Astral Candle of wife dressed with Zodiac brand Oil.*

Position 4   *Red Candle (or Fire of Love brand Candle) dressed with Fire of Love brand Oil.*

Position 5   *Gold Candle (or Glow of Attraction brand Candle) dressed with Glow of Attraction brand Oil.*

Position 6   *Purple Candle (or Conquering Glory brand Candle) dressed with Glow of Attraction brand Oil.*

If desired two symbol candles may be used in this exercise placed along side of candles 2 and 3.

MOVEMENT: Candles 2 and 3 should be moved two inches daily in direction of arrows.

Suggested Bible Reading: The Song of Solomon, Chapter 3.

Devotions: Alternate nights for nine days, one hour each time until satisfied.

EXERCISE 13

TO OVERCOME A BAD HABIT

Position 1-1   *White Crucifix Altar Candles dressed with Hi-Altar brand Oil.*

Position 2   *Black Candle (or Weed of Misfortune brand Candle) to symbolize the bad habit, undressed.*

Positions 3, 4, 5, 6, 7, 8 *White Candles (or Flaming Power brand Candles) dressed with Hi-Altar brand Oil.*

MOVEMENT: Candles 3, 4, 5, 6, 7, 8 should be moved two inches daily in direction of arrows.

Suggested Bible Reading: Psalm No. 25

Devotions: The black Candle is lighted after all the rest and remains lighted *only* while reading the 25th Psalm. When Black Candle is extinguished allow all other candles to burn for one hour thus symbolizing the conquering of the bad habit. Repeat until satisfied.

EXERCISE 14

TO STOP SLANDER

Position 1-1 *White Crucifix Altar Candles dressed with Hi-Altar brand Oil.*

Position 2 *Brown Candle (or Spark of Suspicion brand Candle) dressed with Fiery Command brand Oil.*

Position 3 *Astral Candle of Petitioner dressed with Zodiac brand Oil.*

Position 4 *Light Blue Candle (or Fiery Wall of Protection brand Candle*) dressed with Fiery Wall of Protection brand Oil.*

Positions 5 and 6 *Orchid Candles (or Satan-be-gone brand Candles) dressed with Inflammatory Confusion brand Oil.*

MOVEMENT: Move Candles 5 and 6 two inches daily in direction of arrows.

Suggested Bible Reading. The Second Psalm

Devotions: One hour each evening before retiring until satisfied.

*If preferred the Blue GUARDIAN symbol candle may be used instead of the regulation Fiery Wall of Protection brand Candle.

EXERCISE 15

TO RELIEVE PRESSURE BY AN ENEMY
FOR THOSE WHO ARE IN A SO-CALLED
"CROSSED CONDITION"

Position 1-1 *White Crucifix Altar Candles dressed with Hi-Altar brand Oil.*

Position 2 *Astral Candle of petitioner dressed with Zodiac brand Oil.*

Position 3 *Astral Candle of enemy dressed with Zodiac brand Oil.*

Position 4 *Orchid Candle (or Satan-be-gone brand Candle) dressed with Uncrossing brand Oil.*

Position 5 *Light Blue Candle (or Fiery Wall of Protection brand Candle*) dressed with Fiery Wall of Protection brand Oil.*

Position 6 *Mandrake root in a saucer or incense burner over which incense is burned.*

Suggested Bible Reading. Psalm No. 59
Devotions: One hour daily before retiring until satisfied.

*If preferred the Blue GUARDIAN Symbol Candle may be used instead of he regulation Fiery Wall of Protection brand Candle.

EXERCISE 16

TO ATTAIN SUCCESS

Position 1-1 *White Crucifix Altar Candles dressed with Hi Altar brand Oil.*

Position 2 *Astral Candle of the petitioner dressed with Zodiac brand Oil.*

Position 3 *Orange Candle (or Crown of Success brand Candle) dressed with Crown of Success brand Oil.*

Position 4 *GOLD Candle (or Glow of Attraction brand Candle) dressed with Glow of Attraction brand Oil.*

NOTE:—Devotees usually burn one each of 2, 3 and 4
      candles each day for 9 days.
Suggested Biblical Reading: Psalm of David No. 95
Method: The candles are lighted in the morning, the
      95th Psalm is read, then Candles extinguished.
      After sundown the Candles are relighted and
      allowed to burn out.
NOTE:—If the Success the petitioner has in mind deals with
      MONEY use GREEN Candle (or WEALTHY WAY
      brand Candle) in the No. 3 position.

EXERCISE 17
TO GAIN WHAT ONE DESIRES

This is the same as Exercise 11 except that alongside
the Astral Candle in position "A" is placed a candle to
symbolize the object of one's desires. The following will
give an idea of the color of candle to use. *Crown of Success
brand Oil is used in dressing all candles.*
MONEY—Green Candle (or Wealthy Way brand Candle)
LOVE—Red Candle (or Fire of Love brand Candle)
HAPPINESS—Pink Candles (or Happiness brand Can-
    dles)
GOOD LUCK—Gold Candles (or Lady Luck brand Can-
    dles)
SUCCESS—Orange Candles (or Crown of Success brand
    Candles)
HEALTH—Red Candles (or Radiant Health brand Can-
    dles)
PROSPERITY—Light Green Candles (or Prosperity
    brand Candles)
FORTUNATE DREAMS—Lavendar Candles (or Bene-
    ficial Dream brand Candles)

EXERCISE 18
IN HOPE OF REGAINING or RETAINING HEALTH
*Position 1-1 White Crucifix Altar Candles dressed with
Hi-Altar brand Oil.*

Position 2   *Astral Candle of the petitioner dressed with Zodiac brand Oil.*

Positions 3, 4 and 5 Red Candles (or Radiant Health brand Candles) dressed with Crucible of Courage brand Oil.

Positions 6, 7 and 8 White Candles (or Power Brand Candles) dressed with Crucible of Courage brand Oil.

Movement: Move Candles, 3, 4, 5, 6, 7, 8 in direction of arrows two inches daily.

Suggested Bible Reading: Psalm 38 one day and Psalm 23 on alternate days.

Devotions: Half hour morning and evening until satisfied.

EXERCISE 19

TO LEARN THE TRUTH

Position 1-1 White Crucifix Altar Candles dressed with Hi-Altar brand Oil.

Position 2   *Astral Candle of the petitioner dressed with Zodiac brand Oil.*

Position 3   *White Candle unbranded dressed with Glow of Attraction brand Oil.*

Movement: Move candle No. 3, three inches daily in direction of arrows.

Suggested Biblical Reading: Psalm 117

Devotions: Read the above Psalm thirty-three times. Burn candles for at least one hour daily until satisfied.

EXERCISE 20

TO BRING CONFUSION TO ANOTHER WHO IS THOUGHT TO HAVE CAUSED

UNFAVORABLE VIBRATIONS

Position 1-1 White Crucifix Altar Candles dressed with Hi-Altar brand Oil.

Position 2 *Astral Candle of the petitioner dressed with Zodiac brand Oil.*

Position 3 *DARK Blue Candle (or Inflammatory Confusion brand Candle) dressed with Inflammatory Confusion brand Oil.*

Position 4 *Black Candle (or Weed of Misfortune brand Candle) dressed with Inflammatory Confusion brand Oil.*

Suggested Bible Reading: Psalm No. 70

Devotions: 30 minutes each evening for 9 days before retiring.

The Black Candle *should be extinguished* after reading the seventieth Psalm only once.

EXERCISE 21

TO BREAK UP A LOVE AFFAIR

Position 1-1 *BLACK Crucifix Candles (or Crucifix type Weed of Misfortune brand Candles) dressed with XX Double Cross brand Oil.*

Position 4 *RED Candle (or Fire of Love brand Candle) UNDRESSED to symbolize sterility or barrenness.*

Position 2 *Astral Candle of man involved dressed with with Zodiac brand Oil.*

Position 3 *Astral Candle of woman involved dressed with Zodiac brand Oil.*

Symbol candles may be used alongside candles 2 and 3 if desired.

MOVEMENT: Move No. 2 and No. 3 candles two inches daily in direction of arrows. **DO NOT** move candle 4.

Devotions: Light candles in this order: 4, 2, 3, 1-1 last. Allow 1-1 candles to burn 15 minutes then Extinguish. Burn remaining three candles for one hour longer. Daily devotions until satisfied.

Suggested Bible Reading: The Third Psalm.

TO SOOTHE AND QUIET THE NERVES

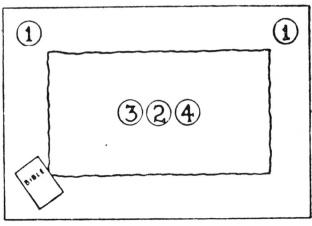

Fig. 33

Position 1-1 *White Crucifix Altar Candles dressed* **with** *Hi-Altar brand Oil.*

Position 2 *Astral Candle of person in nervous condition dressed with Zodiac brand Oil.*

Position 3 *Light Blue or Peaceful Home brand Candle dressed with Fiery Wall of Protection brand Oil.*

Position 4 *Orange Candle or Crucible of Courage brand Candle dressed with Crucible of Courage brand Oil.*

Suggested Bible Reading: Psalm No. 37

Devotions: The Psalm should be read slowly and with careful attention and should be accompanied by a state of calm meditation for at least one hour each day.

THE MAGIC CANDLE
by Charmain Dey
62 pages   **$3.50**

The main object of this book is to help you understand what you are doing, and to create and develop your own techniques and rituals which will surely bring you the results you desire.

It doesn't matter what your religion is. You really don't have to be religious (or anti-religious) at all. Candle burning is a Psychic and Psychological experience, and may compliment your particular faith by arranging your rituals to blend into it. Nevertheless, you need not do anything which you feel is inharmonious with your personal beliefs, as there are countless alternatives.

There are countless authorities and traditions which attempt to tell you precisely what to do in each type of candle-burning ritual or "spell," but few which attempt to explain the reasons why it must be just so. The actual reason is because that is what works best for them — but does it mean anything to you?

The one basic simple fact we can feel sure of is that the act of burning candles does indeed cause an altered state of awareness, producing changes in circumstances. Think of the millions of men and women who have been persuaded and seduced, or extracted promises and proposals, concluded business deals, patched up squabbles, and resolved differences of opinion in the glowing magic of a candlelight supper. And many a birthday wish has come true when all the candles were blown out!

SANTERÍA
African Magic in Latin America
by Migéne Gonzalez-Wippler
181 pages   **$6.95**

Latin American magic, better known in Spanish as Santeria, had its birth in Nigeria, along the banks of the Niger River. This is the country of origin of the Yoruba people, who, among many other African tribes, were brought to the New World by slave traders over four centuries ago. The Yorubas brought with them the colorful mythology of their religion, known in Cuba as lucumi and in Brazil as macumba.

The most important and interesting aspect of the Yoruba culture is their mythology and religious practices. Extensive studies and researches have been made about the Yoruba cult. These studies have shown that the Yoruba pantheon is extremely complex and sophisticated, and strongly reminiscent of the ancient Greeks. Their gods and goddesses, known as orishas, are believable and extraordinarily human in their behavior. The term orisha is of uncertain origin. Some anthropologists believe it is derived from the word asha, meaning religious ceremony. Others claim it is formed of the roots ri ("to see") and sha ("to choose"). There are many orishas in the pantheon. Some authorities say that in Africa their number exceeds six hundred. In Latin America only a few of these are known and paid homage to.

The cult of Santeria is a curious mixture of the magic rites of the Yorubas and the traditions of the Catholic church. All the legends and historical arguments that surround the life of Jesus, Mary, and the Catholic saints are of great important to the santero, as these data serve to delineate the personalities of the saints, making it easier to identify them with the appropriate Yoruba gods. But although the santero often finds his way to the Catholic church for an occasional mass, his sporadic visits are usually prompted by ulterior motives; namely, he may need some holy water for a spell, or a piece of the consecrated host, or maybe some candle wax with which to harm an enemy. For, in spite of the influence of the Catholic church, Santeria is mostly primitive magic, and its roots are deeply buried in the heart of Africa, the ancestral home of the Yoruba people.

RITUALS and SPELLS of SANTERIA
by Migéne Gonzalez-Wippler
134 pages   **$6.95**

Santería is an earth religion. That is, it is a magico-religious system that has its roots in nature and natural forces. Each orisha or saint is identified with a force of nature and with a human interest or endeavor. Changó, for instance, is the god of fire, thunder and lightning, but he is also the symbol of justice and protects his followers against enemies. He also symbolizes passion and virility and is often invoked in works of seduction. Oshún, on the other hand, symbolizes river water, love and marriage. She is essentially archetype of joy and pleasure. Yemaya is identified with the seven seas, but is also the symbol of Motherhood and protects women in their endeavors. Eleggua symbolizes the crossroads, and is the orisha of change and destiny, the one who makes things possible or impossible. He symbolizes the balance of things. Obatala is the father, the symbol of peace and purity. Oya symbolizes the winds and is the owner of the cemetery, the watcher of the doorway between life and death. She is not death, but the awareness of its existence. Oggún is the patron of all metals, and protects farmers, carpenters, butchers, surgeons, mechanics, and all who work with or near metals. He also rules over accidents, which he often causes.

The author of this book has written "Santería" and "Santería Experience." This book takes us further into the practices of Santeria's followers.

THE MASTER BOOK OF CANDLE BURNING
or How to Burn Candles For Every Purpose
by Henri Gamache
96 pages   **$3.50**

"How can I burn candles in a manner which will bring me the most satisfaction and consolation?"

In order to answer that question it is necessary to eliminate all technical, dry and often times torturous historical background. It is necessary to sift and sort every fact, scrutinize every detail, search for the kernel.

It is to be hoped that this volume answers that question in a manner which is satisfactory to the reader. It has been necessary, of course, to include some historical data and other anthropological data in order to better illustrate the symbolism involved in modern candle burning as practised by so many people today.

This data has been accumulated from many sources: it has been culled from literally hundreds of books and articles. The modern rituals outlined here are based upon practices which have been described by mediums, spiritual advisors, evangelists, religious interpreters. neologists and others who should be in a position to know.

It has been the author's desire to interpret and explain the basic symbolism involved in a few typical exercises so that the reader may recognize this symbolism and proceed to develop his own symbolism in accordance with the great beauty and highest ethics of the Art.

THE SANTERIA EXPERIENCE
by Migene Gonzalez-Wippler
228 pages   **$10.95**

"The Santería Experience is an autobiographical account of initiation into a clandestinely-practiced religion. Ms. Gonzalez-Wippler rewards her readers with the raw emotional impact of her personal encounters with the religion as both a researcher and an initiate. She is the first writer to present to an English-speaking audience the full emotional impact and ritual complexities of Santería."
—from the Foreword by Andres I. Perez y Mena

"The Santería Experience fills an important need for a definitive treatise about a religio-magical cult that reputedly has millions of indoctrinated followers in the Caribbean Islands, South America, and Latin American sectors of the United States. Migéne Gonzalez-Wippler is a brilliant narrator whose vivid first-hand descriptions of exotic rituals will be instructive and fascinating to professionals and lay persons alike.

"The Santería Experience, replete with a comprehensive glossary and bibliography, should prove a rewarding experience for all who are intrigued by the advantages and pitfalls of this widespread, mind-expanding phemomenon."

—Stanley R. Dean, M.D.
author/editor of
Psychiatry and Mysticism

HELPING YOURSELF WITH SELECTED PRAYERS
an Original Publications Collection
68 pages   **$3.95**

In publishing this book, Original Products Company is responding to a demand for an English version of many popular prayers formerly available only in Spanish.

HELPING YOURSELF WITH SELECTED PRAYERS provides the English translation for over one hundred prayers of various religious beliefs, spiritualism and superstition: many are what might simply be called folk prayers. **HELPING YOURSELF WITH SELECTED PRAYERS** is a collection of those prayers most often requested by the English reading public.

THE WITCH'S FORMULARY and SPELLBOOK
by Tarostar

96 pages   **$6.95**

Modern American practice in the Occult Arts has borrowed heavily from the Craft's Sister Religion, which has come to be called Voodoo. The spells, ingredients and names for many things in the present day practice in the United States, have come from the Tradition of Magic brought to the New World by the African Slave.

The religious aspects of Voodoo, as practiced in the Islands of the West Indies, was filtered out and only the magic and sorcery of its metaphysical side were kept.

The spells of the Old New Orleans Tradition have, therefore become almost standard American "de rigeur" and are widely sold through most Occult Supply Shops in this Country.

Cultural origin of anything is not important to the modern Practitioner of the Ars Magica in so far as magical efficacy is concerned. Universal Occult Principles are involved and applied by all Metaphysical Systems regardless of ethnic background.

A Shaman in Lappland, a Mambo in Haiti, a Dianic Witch or a Ceremonial Wizard seem to be of the same metaphysical Family. Success in the works of the Great Art is the prime consideration.

Some manufacturers offer pre-made occult products, but the customer is never aware of what the ingredients are.

When buying from an Occult Shop, make certain they mix and make their own at the correct astrological time and with proper magical solemnity. If they do not and only offer factory made items, it is best to mix your own.

A good Witch is a Traditionalist and would feel hand made materia magica is always more effective.

In olden times herbs were gathered right from Nature and properly applied. Today, in this Age of Spiritual Winter, and isolation from Dame Nature, in this Culture of Over-Specialization, the Hand Crafter is looked upon as an oddity.

That, however, has never daunted the true Witch. He/she has never turned away from Dame Nature even in the concrete Nightmares this World has become. He/she still....worketh the Ancient Magic in the traditional way.

THIS BE WITCHES WORK

THE NEW REVISED SIXTH and SEVENTH BOOKS OF MOSES and THE MAGICAL USES OF THE PSALMS
Edited by Migene Gonzalez-Wippler
219 pages $6.95

The Sixth and Seventh Books of Moses was originally published in Stutgart, Germany, in 1849. Its author, a German author by the name of Johann Scheibel, is shrouded in mystery.

The author claimed that the seals and invocations given in the book came from ancient Hebrew sources, particularly the Talmud. It is not sure whether or not his claims were based on truth, although Talmudic scholars will probably deny that there are any references in Talmudic literature to the Sixth and Seventh Books of Moses.

While the original source of the book will probably never be ascertained, its popularity and durability can hardly be denied. This revised edition is an attempt at the reorganization of a work, long hailed by occult masters as a valuable tool in the study and practice of Kabbalistic magic.

It is hoped that this new edition will make the teachings of this venerable work attainable to many readers who up to now were unable to understand it. Undoubtedly, much of the material herein is of little value to the student because of its adulterated nature, but those who are able to glean the gold from the chaff will benefit vastly from this work. If they can fulfill this task, I will consider my humble efforts amply rewarded.

Migene Gonzalez-Wippler

SPIRITUAL CLEANSING
A Handbook of Psychic Protection
by Draja Mickaharic
97 pages $5.95

This book is a manual of psychic first aid, written to help you clean your spiritual atmosphere and to protect yourself in your environment.

Everyone, at some time or another, has met an individual who seems to be surrounded with negativity, or has visit a place that seems imbued with "bad vibrations." removing these negative vibrations is what spiritual cleansing is all about.

With this book you will be able to solve most of the problems of day to day negativity that may be encountered with people, places and things. It teaches how to clean away the psychic drudge in your environment, how to clean the previous tenant's vibrations out of your house or apartment, how to remove vibrations from secondhand furniture or clothing, how to cleanse your own aura. The author's "household formulas" include recipes for herb, nut and flower baths for healing, reducing tension, increasing mental acuity, bringing love into your life, or even for economic improvement. He shows how to use incense and flowers to sweeten the home and clear the air after arguments. He discusses ways of using sea salt to help invalids or children, and the efficacy of eggs to ease physical pain and for protection while asleep.

These simple and effective solutions to common psychic problems are presented in a way that allows the reader to take care of his environment without spending years studying magic.

THE MASTER KEY TO OCCULT SECRETS
by Henri Gamache
84 pages   **$4.95**

It has taken me over three years to gather the material which is presented in this Document, which, I must confess IS presented solely because in it can be found the answers to the many, many questions which have been put to me during that time.

All of the customs, practices, rituals, amulets, sumans, fetiches, prayers, mantrams and other information given in this Document I attest to being accurate and authentic and for proof I have in all instances, indicated the sources, origins and authorities.

Moreover, all of the customs, rituals and nostrums included in this study are being practiced by people in these United States and neighboring Islands today, origins and authorities.

Thus, from the point of view of the student of Religion Anthropology, Sociology, the Occult or Esoteric Arts, I believe it to be a valuable contribution since it presents truthfully the lengths to which humanity will extend itself in an endeavor to gain what its heart desires, even in the face of almost insurmountable obstacles.

Just so long as people cling to customs such as these — and attain, by a Strange Fate, the things they desire — the "Age of Miracles, will not pass.

Henri Gamache

MYSTERY OF THE LONG LOST
8th, 9th & 10th
BOOKS OF MOSES
by Henri Gamache
103 pages $3.50

The object of this present volume is to serve a three-fold purpose:

First, to present an abbreviated, humanized biography of the Man Moses in such form as to make him seem alive rather than a cold, mythical personage out of a fairy tale.

Second, there are some who may criticize the title of this book, saying that only the first five Books of the Old Testament belong to Moses; that there were no Sixth and Seventh Books of Moses, nor any additonal books by the Great Man.

If you have been inclined to this view, Book Two of this volume may give food for thought. The conclusions set forth are Not my own but the consensus of opinions arrived at independently by many learned students of religion of the Ancient Nation of Israel and of the Old and New Testaments. From this testimony it can be concluded that it is just as accurate to say that Moses wrote ten books as it is to limit him to the authorship of only the first five books of the Old Testament.

Third, in Book Three of this volume, which your author has entitled: "The Book of Miscellaney," have been assembled many of the nostrums used in the period under discussion. These are presented so that the reader may have a greater insight into the character of these people; that their everyday habits may be analyzed; that their fundamentally religious instincts may be measured to some degree. Finally, they are presented for comparison with many customs, superstitions, traditions, prayers and nostrums which many readers will recognize as bearing a striking similarity to those which exist and are practised even today.

When all has been summed up it will be seen that despite all of our modern science, all of our book learning, all of the changes which have been brought about in the past 4000 years, human nature itself changes not at all and those ancients of the misty past are but our next door neighbors today.

Henri Gamache